Modern
Asian Baking
at Home

Essential Sweet
and Savory Recipes
for Milk Bread, Mochi,
Mooncakes, and More

—

Inspired by the
Subtle Asian Baking
Community

Modern Asian Baking at Home

Kat Lieu

Founder, @subtleasian.baking

QUARRY

Brimming with creative inspiration, how-to projects, and useful information to enrich your everyday life, quarto.com is a favorite destination for those pursuing their interests and passions.

First Published in 2022 by Quarry Books,
an imprint of The Quarto Group,
100 Cummings Center, Suite 265-D
Beverly, MA 01915, USA.
—
T (978) 282-9590 / F (978) 283-2742
Quarto.com

Quarry Books titles are also available at discount for retail, wholesale, promotional, and bulk purchase. For details, contact the Special Sales Manager by email at specialsales@quarto.com or by mail at The Quarto Group, Attn: Special Sales Manager, 100 Cummings Center, Suite 265-D, Beverly, MA 01915, USA.

10 9 8 7 6 5 4 3 2 1

ISBN: 978-0-7603-7428-3

Digital edition published in 2022
eISBN: 978-0-7603-7429-0

Library of Congress Cataloging-in-Publication Data

Names: Lieu, Kat, author.
Title: Modern Asian baking at home : essential sweet and savory recipes for milk bread, mooncakes, mochi, and more ; inspired by the subtle Asian baking community / Kat Lieu, founder, @subtleasian.baking.
Description: Beverly, MA : Quarry Books, 2022. | Includes index. | Summary: "Inspired by the global "Subtle Asian" community, Modern Asian Baking at Home features exciting, contemporary Asian-inspired ingredients and techniques bakers of all levels will want to add to their repertoires"--Provided by publisher.
Identifiers: LCCN 2021055202 (print) | LCCN 2021055203 (ebook) | ISBN 9780760374283 (board) | ISBN 9780760374290 (ebook)
Subjects: LCSH: Baking. | Cooking, Asian. | LCGFT: Cookbooks.
Classification: LCC TX763 .L54 2022 (print) | LCC TX763 (ebook) | DDC 641.81/5--dc23/eng/20211122
LC record available at https://lccn.loc.gov/2021055202
LC ebook record available at https://lccn.loc.gov/2021055203

Design: Timothy Samara
Photography: Nicole Soper Photography except images on pages 8 and 18 are Jake Young

Printed in Singapore

I dedicate this book to you (the reader), my beloved family, friends, the SAB community, and Mom and Dad.

—

Dad, if only we had more time together, I'd make all these treats for you.

Contents

Introduction

I'd like to welcome you to the extraordinary world of modern Asian baking. Wait. Let's start over. I want to thank you for welcoming this book and me into your home. It's an incredible honor to be here. My eyes are flooding as I write this because I still can't believe I've authored an entire cookbook on Asian baking! "But you're not classically trained, *Kalai,*" my mom said to me in Cantonese when I told her I had a book deal. She's right (and when is she not?). I'm just a self-taught home baker with an insatiable thirst for learning and improving, and hey, I'm proud of that fact.

I have another confession to make. As a child, I thought Asians didn't bake. Clean pots and pans were permanent residents in our oven. Whenever my mom made Chinese sweets and desserts, she steamed, boiled, or fried her ingredients. In 2009, when my parents sold the house where we lived for more than two decades, the oven was pristine. I kid you not.

For more than thirty years, I called South Brooklyn my home. There's at least one Asian bakery or restaurant on every block of 86th Street by Bay Parkway. Now settled in the quiet suburbs of Seattle, I've driven long distances to buy my favorite Asian comfort foods. It's quite a bummer because I don't particularly like to drive. Having a kitchen big enough to allow my oven to be used as an oven instead of storage space, I felt a strong bite from the baking bug. I dreamed of baking everything I loved to eat but found challenging to easily procure locally: milk bread, mooncakes, mochi, and of course, the notoriously difficult-to-perfect Japanese cheesecake.

I wanted to, no, *needed* to bake (don't laugh) the Asian way. Dazed in my then-empty kitchen, I had no idea where and how to begin. What Asian goodies should I bake first? Where could I find high-quality Asian baking recipes? I scoured the web for a comprehensive collection of Asian baking recipes; alas, my searches came up short. I had hit a roadblock to Asian baking. My first bake in my new kitchen was a Western creation. If you guessed banana bread, you're right. Cue the eye roll.

I saw a need for an online community where beginner and experienced home bakers could share, search for, and obsess over Asian baking. I knew I had to build this community, one that would bridge cultures and help people collaborate, innovate, learn, and get instant inspiration. On May 24, 2020, I launched Subtle Asian Baking (SAB), an inclusive and diverse Asian baking group on Facebook. SAB welcomed more than 100,000 members worldwide within ten months of inception. SAB members have curated and shared thousands of essential Asian sweet and savory baking recipes, along with countless heartwarming stories.

And why did I name the group Subtle Asian Baking? One, because I love the Subtle Asian communities online. And two, because there are so many clever, subtle methods and techniques to baking the Asian way.

> "Subtle Asian Baking is no longer just a small community of bakers swapping recipes, but a movement for culinary innovation."
>
> JESSICA WEI · EATER.COM

Thanks to the SAB community, I have grown tremendously as a home baker and recipe developer. I'm thrilled to share what I've learned with you in this book. The recipes I've included are a mix of my inventions and inspirations from SAB members. Some recipes are unique and brand-new, such as my Dreamy Matcha Basque Cheesecake (page 80) and Crème Brûlée Mille-Crêpes Cake (page 90). Some are old-world, like *tanghulu* fruits (page 42) and *tangyuan* (page 126). All the recipes come from our hearts and homes. I sincerely hope this book brings you joy as you bake delicious and crave-worthy foods to enjoy at home and share with your neighbors and loved ones.

Whether you're a new, experienced, classically trained, or self-taught home baker (like me!), and regardless of whether you're Asian or not, you'll find a recipe to obsess over, and at least one (or two, or three, or more) that you'll make over and over again. Let this book be your baking buddy as you work with transformative ingredients from East and Southeast Asia, such as matcha, black sesame, and ube. With matcha's subtle nutty and bitter notes, we'll make not-too-sweet and *umamiful* desserts, such as Monstrous Matcha Miso Cookies (page 52) and Black Sesame Mochi Beignets (page 68). Using ube, we'll make beautifully vibrant and purple Soft Crumb Ube White Chocolate Scones (page 70) and the Greatest Ube Halaya Jam (page 28) to spread over your Super Easy Milk Bread (page 100).

Exciting ingredients, different techniques, and interesting textures differentiate Asian baking from Western baking. Have you ever chewed boba and felt an ASMR (autonomous sensory meridian response) level of satisfaction? Boba pearls with a hearty chew are *QQ,* a darling texture and mouthfeel of Taiwan. (QQ is possibly short for *k'iu,* a word that means bouncy in the Taiwanese dialect Hokkien.) If you've never had boba (doubtful, but possible), don't worry! We'll make home-made boba using just three ingredients (page 32). Plus, when we make quick mochi in the microwave (page 24), you'll see how easy it is to achieve the remarkable and alluring texture that is QQ.

Another Asian baking texture—and this one is a favorite of mine—is airiness. You'll know you're having an Asian cake when you sink your teeth into my favorite dessert of all time, the light Cottony Japanese Cheesecake (page 82).

I hope you're excited and ready to steam, fry, boil, and bake your way through this straight-from-the-heart collection of recipes. Have fun, get a little messy, and splatter batter and condensed milk all over this book! It's meant to be scribbled on, dog-eared, and stained. Writing this book, I imagined it to be your loyal companion and a guide as you embark on a baking adventure full of innovation and discovery. You'll add mochi boba to ice pops (page 156), make naan bread with sourdough starter (page 108), and spice up a delicious flour-less chocolate cake with *gochujang* (page 78)!

Roll up your sleeves, take off your shoes, and explore the magical world of modern Asian baking. The best part? No passports or packing required when you can bake the Asian way, right at home.

The Asian Pantry
*Ingredients
and Recipe Notes*

Some ingredients used in this book may seem unfamiliar. Luckily, in our modern world, you can easily find these ingredients online or at your local Asian market or grocery store.

BLACK SESAME Black sesame turns foods dark gray and adds a pleasant nutty and toasty flavor. To make black sesame powder, you can toast and grind black sesame seeds.

CALAMANSI Green and tart like lime, this small citrus hails from the Philippines. Calamansi is commonly used to make cocktails, juices, and sauces as it adds a pop of bright flavor and tang.

FIVE-SPICE POWDER Commonly used in Chinese and Taiwanese cuisine, five-spice powder consists of five different spices (such as cloves, fennel, star anise, cinnamon, and gingerroot) encompassing the taste spectrum: umami, salty, sweet, bitter, and sour.

GLUTINOUS RICE FLOUR Also known as sweet rice flour, this gluten-free and starchy flour is efficient as a thickening agent. It's perfect for making QQ foods such as mochi. If you come across *shiratamako* and *mochiko* glutinous rice flour, choose shiratamako, especially when making *dango,* because it's easier to work with. (Using either one is okay to make the recipes in this book, and mochiko is easier to find.)

GOCHUJANG This popular Korean condiment consists of fermented soybean powder and glutinous rice powder mixed with red chili, salt, and *yeotgireum* (barley malt powder). It's not a one-note hot sauce and can be a surprisingly delicious addition to your savory and sweet creations, especially when chocolate is involved.

JUJUBES Jujubes are red dates, or Chinese dates, often found packaged and dried in Asian markets. Jujubes are used to sweeten soups and add a pop of color to desserts.

MATCHA Made from dried, shade-grown green tea leaves, matcha colors food an aesthetic grassy green and adds vegetal umami. For the recipes in this book, I recommend using culinary grade matcha. Ceremonial grade matcha, although more beautifully green, is costly and is best enjoyed and most flavorful when whisked into green tea.

MISO Miso is a salty, earthy, umamiful paste made from fermented soybeans. Like salt, miso can enhance flavors and balance foods, especially sweets. For savory recipes, I recommend using red or yellow miso. I recommend using white (sweet) miso for the sweet recipes in this book, as it is more delicate and milder than its red and yellow counterparts, due to a shorter fermentation time.

PANDAN A fragrant plant from Southeast Asia, its aromatic leaves are often used to flavor foods and color them vibrantly green. Some call pandan the "Asian vanilla extract." For the recipes in this book, I recommend using a green-colored pandan extract. Feel free to make pandan extract from scratch by blending pandan leaves with water and straining the mixture.

PANKO Flaky breadcrumbs made from crustless white milk bread, panko is often used in Japanese and Asian cooking and baking. When fried, a panko crust is crispy and light.

RICE FLOUR Rice flour is a gluten-free flour made from grinding uncooked medium- and long-grain rice. It's great as a thickening agent and a wheat flour substitute. Unlike glutinous rice flour, however, you won't be able to make mochi or other QQ treats with rice flour.

SOY SAUCE Soy sauce, made from fermented soybeans, is known for its saltiness and strong umami flavor. Try using soy sauce to make addictive salty caramels and salty-sweet sauces for your desserts.

TAPIOCA (STARCH) FLOUR This gluten-free starchy flour comes from cassava roots. It is versatile and has a subtle sweetness. Like glutinous rice flour, you can use tapioca flour to thicken foods and make your bakes QQ.

TOFU Tofu can easily replace eggs in your bakes. Made from coagulated soy milk that has never formed curds, silken tofu is delicate and soft.

UBE This Filipino purple yam is sweet and tastes like a nutty vanilla coconut. Ube is versatile and transformative as an ingredient as it turns food beautifully purple. For my bakes to achieve an eye-grabbing vibrant purple, I don't shy away from using ube extract.

RECIPE NOTES

Use the following ingredients unless otherwise specified:

All eggs are large (about 2 ounces, or 50 g, each).

All dairy milk is full-fat. (Dairy-free alternatives are listed.)

All butter is unsalted.

All salt is non-iodized kosher or table salt.

All food coloring is gel.

For consistency and accuracy, all ingredients used in this book's recipes, including liquids, are measured in grams with a digital kitchen scale.

Techniques

Here you'll find valuable techniques along with helpful pictures to refer back to as needed when you go through the recipes in this book.

ALL ABOUT STEAMING

Steaming is a great way to cook and reheat food. I highly recommend having a wok, a steamer rack, and one to two 8- to 10-inch (20.5 to 25.5 cm) bamboo steamers at home.

To steam, place a steamer rack on the bottom of a wok (or large pot or heavy saucepan) and fill with water that reaches the top of the steamer rack. Boil the water, place the steamer on the rack, cover with the lid, and let the steam from the continuously boiling water do the cooking. Replenish with hot water, as needed.

When using bamboo steamers, be sure to line them with perforated parchment paper. You can steam food (such as dumplings, buns, baos, dim sum, and even a whole fish) directly on top of the parchment paper in the steamer.

When steaming cakes, such as nian gao (page 130) or the skin of the snowy mooncake (page 128), that require a separate heat-proof container, place a steamer rack or insert into a large saucepan. Fill the saucepan with water until it reaches the top of the steamer rack. Boil the water. Then place the food you're about to steam in a heatproof container and cover with aluminum foil. Place the container on top of the steamer rack. Cover the saucepan with a lid. Let the steam from the boiling water cook the food in the container.

If you don't have a steamer rack, here's a hack: Crumple three sheets of aluminum foil into three balls. Set them on the bottom of the wok, pot, or saucepan in a triangular array and level the container with the food you're about to steam on top of the three aluminum balls.

Please always be careful when steaming food. Never touch steam or place your face near steam.

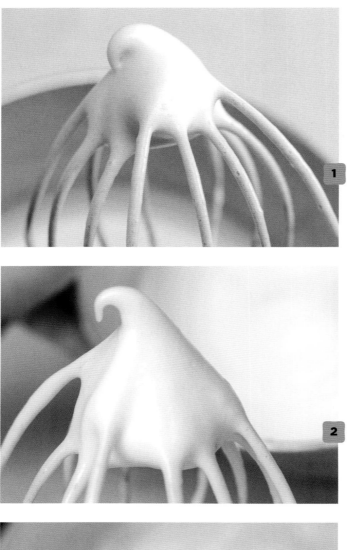

BEATING EGG WHITES

Using a stand mixer or hand mixer, beat room-temperature egg whites and a stabilizing acid (like vinegar, cream of tartar, or lemon juice) on medium-high speed until foamy and opaque, a few minutes. Lower the speed to add the sugar in increments. Turn the speed back to medium-high.

For soft peaks, beat until the meringue starts to hold its shape. When the whisk attachment is upside down, soft peaks will droop, slouch, and quickly melt back into the meringue (Fig. 1).

For firm (or medium) peaks, continue to beat the meringue until the peak holds its shape better. When you flip the whisk upside down this time, the peak, while more distinct, will still droop and fold back on itself (Fig. 2).

For stiff peaks, whip the meringue until glossy and tripled in volume. The peak will be tall, sharp, and pointing upward (Fig 3).

Overbeaten egg whites will be clumpy, like curds.

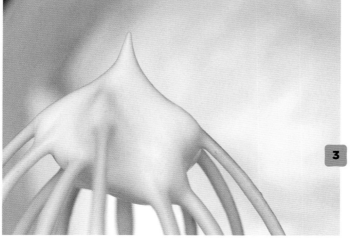

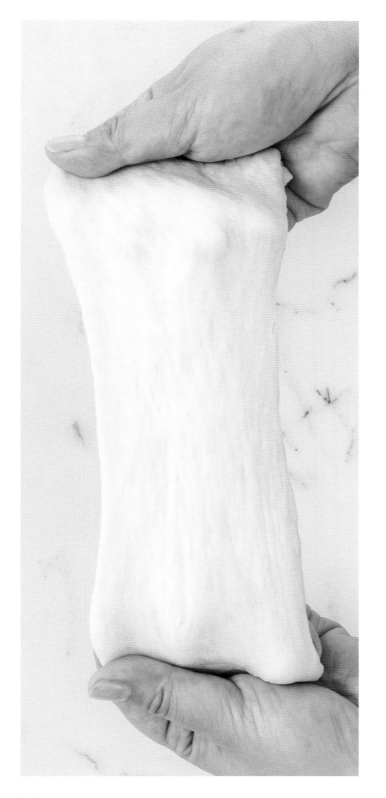

PERFORMING THE WINDOWPANE TEST

Shape a small piece of dough into a ball and flatten it between your palms. Gently stretch until thin. If it can become translucent (like a windowpane) before tearing, it's well kneaded. At that point, you can let the dough rest and rise. If the dough tears or is very soft, wet, and not elastic, add a little bit more bread flour and continue to knead the dough. Perform the test again.

If the dough barely stretches and is too tough, it's over-kneaded. You can still salvage it with an extended resting time, such as 90 minutes instead of 60 minutes, during the first rise.

RISING THE DOUGH

It's best to allow the dough to rise at a warm temperature, usually in the same bowl the dough was mixed in.

I also love my oven's proof mode. A damp, lint-free towel over the bowl keeps the dough nice and happy as it rises.

Before the first rise, the dough should be soft and elastic. It rises successfully when it can stretch, yet the gluten strands are still strong enough to contain yeast farts (or carbon dioxide, if you want to be scientific about it) as the yeast feast on the carbohydrates in the dough (the leavening process).

—

Please note that not every bread dough needs to or will pass the windowpane test.

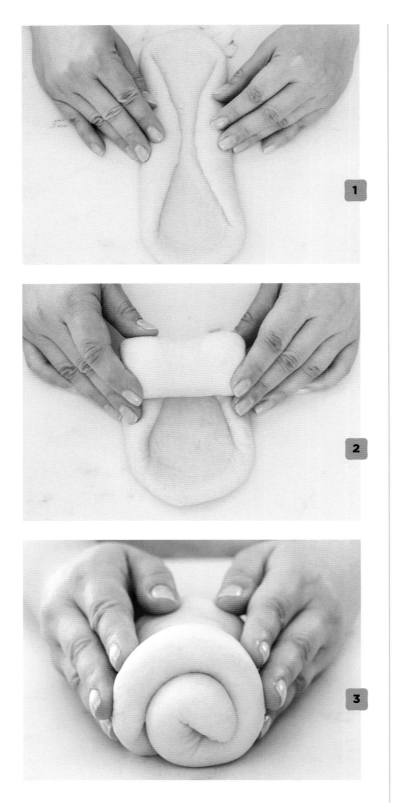

SHAPING MILK BREAD DOUGH

To shape bread loaves, use a rolling pin to roll each piece of dough into a long oval. Fold in the left and right sides of each piece of dough toward the center to make a skinnier piece of dough (Fig. 1). Starting from the bottom, roll each piece of dough upward and away from you (Fig. 2). You should end up with a roll that looks like Figure 3. Place the rolled dough, seam-side down and side by side, in a prepared loaf pan.

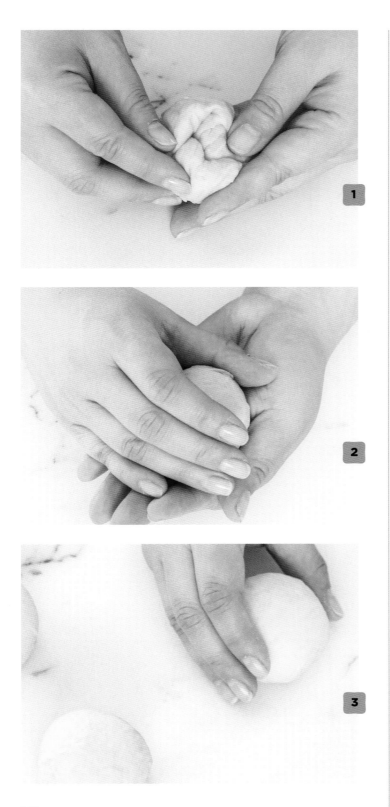

SHAPING MILK BREAD BUNS

Divide the dough into equal pieces. After the first rise and before proofing, shape each piece of dough into a ball and flatten into a disc. Tuck the disc into itself by pinching in the dough from all sides into the middle (Fig. 1). This creates a round shape (Fig. 2). Place the ball seam-side down on the work surface. With your hand cupping the ball, roll in a circular motion to firmly shape the ball (Fig. 3).

To make a *football-shaped* bun, roll each piece of dough into a flat and long oval. Roll the oval into a tight log and pinch in the seams. Pinch in the two ends and shape into a football.

Basics and Confections

It may come as a surprise to you that we use the oven for only three dishes in this section. (No, it's not because I've stuffed my oven with pots and pans, LOL.) The recipes here showcase techniques differentiating Asian baking from Western baking. We'll use a microwave to quickly make mochi (page 24) and homemade boba (page 32). We'll use steam to make memory foam–like buns (page 34). We'll use a frying pan to make flaky Night Market Scallion Pancakes (page 30), just like ones you'd find at the night markets across Asia.

The recipes here also introduce a texture or ingredient unique to Asian baking. For example, with my Greatest Ube Halaya Jam recipe (page 28), we'll make a lovely purple spread using a special ingredient from the Philippines: ube.

We'll also be making some of my favorite Asian confections, such as the trendy and modern Chewy Taiwanese Snowflake Crisps (page 44). Some confections are rich with history and tradition, such as *hanami dango* (page 48) and tanghulu fruits (page 42). Be sure to share these tasty treats with your family and friends. You'll sweeten their day and wow them for sure.

Dear friend, I have so many incredible modern Asian baking recipes to share with you. Let's start with some of my favorites. I hope all the recipes here will become your favorite and go-to recipes too.

To change the color of your mochi, mix in food coloring gel or colored food powders.

Quick Microwave Mochi

Mochi (rice cake) was once considered a sacred food in Japan. Now it is eaten all year round. When I traveled across Japan, I loved sampling many varieties of mochi: *daifuku, warabimochi, sakuramochi*— I can go into detail about each type, but then I'll have to write a second book!

Feel free to experiment with this recipe. Flatten the mochi dough into discs and then fill them with your favorite savory or sweet fillings, like ice cream. I know you'll have so *mochi* fun. (Yes, I had to go there.)

RECIPE SPECS

FOR LINING THE BAKING SHEET

¼ cup (32 g) cornstarch

1 tablespoon (8 g) confectioners' sugar

FOR THE MOCHI

1 cup (120 g) glutinous rice flour

½ cup (60 g) confectioners' sugar, adjust to taste

1 tablespoon (8 g) cornstarch

1 cup (235 g) water (or milk for a creamier mochi)

1 tablespoon (14 g) butter, softened

FOR THE OPTIONAL TOPPINGS

1 tablespoon (5 g) cocoa powder or (6 g) matcha

1 tablespoon (20 g) honey or (19 g) sweetened condensed milk

1 In a frying pan, toast the cornstarch over medium-low heat for a few minutes to kill any bacteria. Spread evenly over a parchment paper-lined baking sheet. Add the confectioners' sugar. You'll use this later to coat the mochi.

2 *Make the mochi.* Whisk all the mochi ingredients in a microwave-safe bowl until combined and not lumpy. Microwave on high power for 1 to 2 minutes. Mix until evenly combined. Microwave for another minute and mix again. If there are any wet parts left, microwave for an additional minute. The mochi is ready when it is slightly translucent, cohesive, and evenly cooked. Add the butter and mix thoroughly.

3 Cover and cool until the mochi is no longer too hot to touch, about 8 minutes.

4 Wear food-safe gloves. Knead and stretch the mochi for about 15 seconds. It'll be sticky.

(Stop here if you are using the mochi in another recipe; otherwise, continue.)

5 Transfer the mochi to the prepared baking sheet. Coat lightly with the cornstarch and sugar mixture.

6 Roll the mochi into a log. Divide the log into eight even pieces. Working one at a time, flatten each piece into a disc. Tuck the disc onto itself by pinching in the dough from all sides into the middle. This creates a round shape. Place the mochi ball seam-side down on the work surface. With your fingers cupping the mochi ball, roll in a circular motion to firmly shape the ball. You can also roll the ball between your palms. Note the mochi may flatten a bit and not hold its shape well without any filling, and that's okay. Perfection is overrated anyway.

7 Place on a serving plate. Dust with matcha or cocoa powder. For added sweetness, drizzle with honey or condensed milk.

8 Store in an airtight container and eat within 2 days.

Did you know you can also make this mochi in a saucepan or with steam? Visit my website modernasianbaking.com *to learn more.*

PREP TIME	20 MINUTES
COOK TIME	A FEW MINUTES
YIELD	8 PIECES

Fluffy Japanese Soufflé Pancakes

A few years ago, I asked Jake (my ~~chauffeur~~ husband) to drive from Seattle to Vancouver just so I could try soufflé pancakes at Night Market Vancouver. The pancakes did not disappoint! They were airy, jiggly, and super Instagrammable. Because I couldn't keep asking Jake to drive to Vancouver, I had to make my own fluffy Japanese pancakes at home.

Note: Don't worry when you're whisking and folding the meringue into the pancake batter. As with the chiffon and airy cakes in this book, the meringue here must be well incorporated into the batter in order for you to make fluffy, tall, and light Japanese pancakes.

RECIPE SPECS

FOR THE
PANCAKE BATTER

2 tablespoons (30 g) milk or buttermilk

2 egg yolks (about 1½ ounces, or 40 g)

1 teaspoon vanilla extract

About 2 tablespoons (15 g) all-purpose flour

Pinch of baking powder

1 teaspoon cornstarch

Pinch of salt

Pinch of ground nutmeg (optional)

FOR THE STIFF PEAKS MERINGUE

2 egg whites (about 2 ounces, or 60 g), room temperature

¼ teaspoon cream of tartar or ½ teaspoon of white vinegar

1½ tablespoons (20 g) granulated sugar

OTHER INGREDIENTS

2 tablespoons (30 g) water, divided

Confectioners' sugar for dusting (optional)

FOR THE OPTIONAL TOPPINGS

Sliced fruits

Sweetened condensed milk

Syrup

Honey

1 Lightly grease a large frying pan.

2 *Make the pancake batter.* In a large bowl, whisk together all the pancake batter ingredients until combined and smooth. Set aside.

3 *Make the stiff peaks meringue (see technique on page 18).* Add one-third of the meringue to the pancake batter and gently fold until combined. Repeat with another third of the meringue. Use a flexible spatula to fold the last third of the meringue into the batter. The resulting batter should be very thick and smooth like a fluffy, creamy custard.

4 Transfer the batter to a piping bag. (Alternatively, you can use a cookie scoop or large spoon to scoop batter into the pan. Or you can cook the pancakes in 3 inch [7.5 cm] greased ring molds, resulting in the pancakes as pictured.) In the pan over low to medium-low heat, pipe three even pancakes, each about 3 inches (7.5 cm) in diameter and ¼ inch (1.3 cm) in height. They will spread a little, so space them apart as much as you can. Add more batter on top of each pancake, until all three pancakes are tall. Drizzle 1 tablespoon (15 g) of water onto the pan, surrounding the pancakes. Cover the pan with a lid (preferably a domed one) and cook for 6 to 7 minutes. Slowly remove the lid and carefully flip the pancakes. If the pancakes appear too wet, cook for another minute before flipping. Add the last tablespoon (15 g) of water around the pancakes, cover the pan again, and cook the pancakes for another 6 minutes. Both sides should be golden brown and not burnt.

5 Once removed from heat, the pancakes will deflate, but not dramatically. Top with the toppings of your choice. I like them loaded with a mountain of whipped cream and a dusting of matcha.

PREP TIME	**15 MINUTES**
COOK TIME	**10 TO 12 MINUTES**
YIELD	**3 PANCAKES**

Greatest Ube Halaya Jam

According to recipe tester Jen Lee, this ube halaya jam is one of the most delicious things she's ever tasted. She raved about the lovely umami and salt notes from the miso, the freshness from the lemon, and the pleasant sweetness from the three different kinds of milk and the ube.

Spread this jam generously over your milk bread and crackers or use it to make custards, diplomat creams, *halo-halo*, mooncake filling, Mochi-Stuffed Ube Crinkle Cookies (page 132), and Ube Butter Mochi (page 54).

I named this recipe the "Greatest Ube Halaya Jam" as it is adapted from one by Sheldon Lynn (@sheldoskitchen on Instagram), a SAB member and contestant on season 4 of *The Great Canadian Baking Show*. Thank you, Sheldon, for the inspiration!

About 3 to 4 medium-sized ube (1 pound, or 450 g)

¾ cup (175 g) full-fat coconut milk

¾ cup (230 g) sweetened condensed milk

¾ cup (175 g) evaporated milk

½ cup (115 g) packed dark brown sugar

1 teaspoon miso

½ cup (1 stick, or 112 g) butter

1 tablespoon (15 g) lemon or calamansi juice

A few drops of purple food coloring gel or ½ to 1 teaspoon ube extract (optional)

1 Vigorously scrub and wash the ube. Use a fork to poke holes all over them. Don't dry the ube. Instead, spray or sprinkle some water over them. Microwave on high power for 3 minutes. Carefully turn the ube and microwave for another 4 to 5 minutes. Cool before peeling and cutting into cubes.

2 Using a blender (or an immersion blender), blend the ube, coconut milk, condensed milk, evaporated milk, dark brown sugar, and miso until smooth and homogeneous.

3 Transfer the mixture to a heavy saucepan. Over medium-high heat and while continuously stirring, bring to a boil. Reduce the heat to medium-low and cook for about 40 minutes, occasionally stirring. Meanwhile, in a saucepan over medium heat, heat the butter, while occasionally stirring it, for about 8 minutes, until nutty brown bits form and the butter is a deep golden brown. Set aside for now but keep within reach. When the ube mixture thickens and the jam pulls away from the pot when you're stirring, add the lemon juice, vanilla extract, brown butter, and the optional food coloring or ube extract and stir until homogeneous. Once thickened to your desired jammy consistency, remove from the heat and cool completely. Don't overcook. The ube halaya jam will thicken more once cooled.

4 Store in the fridge and consume within a few days. Freeze in an airtight container to keep for up to 3 months.

Instead of microwaving the ube, you can boil it for about 25 minutes, or until tender. If you cannot find ube, you may use purple sweet potatoes (or Okinawan sweet potatoes) instead.

PREP TIME	25 MINUTES
COOK TIME	40 TO 60 MINUTES
YIELD	1 LARGE JAR

Scallion pancake masters, such as Martin Yan and Wu Gencheng of Shanghai's A Da cōngyóubǐng, bake scallion pancakes for a few minutes immediately after frying them.

Night Market Scallion Pancakes

These scallion pancakes are just as addictive, crispy, and flaky as the ones you'd find freshly made in night markets across Asia. I adapted the recipe from a scallion pancake master, chef Martin Yan. As a child, I would religiously watch reruns of Martin's show, *Yan Can Cook*. In fact, I believe the first time I worked with dough on my own was when I made Martin's scallion pancakes while watching his show! Hashtag #representationmatters.

Enjoy these pancakes as a snack or appetizer, plain or dipped in sauce.

FOR THE PANCAKE DOUGH

2 cups (250 g) all-purpose flour

¼ teaspoon salt

½ cup (120 g) boiling water

¼ cup (60 g) cold water

About 5 to 6 scallions (¾ cup, or 75 g), minced

FOR THE ROUX

About ½ cup (60 g) all-purpose flour

¼ cup (60 g) neutral oil or melted lard

1 teaspoon sesame oil (optional)

1 teaspoon chicken or mushroom bouillon powder (optional)

FOR THE DIPPING SAUCE

2 tablespoons (30 g) soy sauce

2 tablespoons (30 g) Chinkiang or black vinegar

½ teaspoon granulated or brown sugar

1 tablespoon (10 g) minced garlic or shallots

½ teaspoon chili or Szechuan peppercorn oil (optional)

1 *Make the pancake dough.* In a stand mixer fitted with the dough hook attachment (or by hand with a wooden spoon, flexible spatula, or chopsticks), mix the flour and salt. Carefully add the boiling water and mix. Add the cold water and mix just until a ball of dough forms. Cover and rest for 2 hours. You can also refrigerate the dough overnight. (In that case, allow the dough to soften at room temperature before rolling it out.)

2 *Make the roux.* Whisk all the roux ingredients in a saucepan until well incorporated. Cook over medium heat until the mixture simmers. Cool completely.

3 Flour your hands and knead the dough for a few seconds. Roll into a rectangle about 20 x 10 inches (51 x 25.5 cm) in size. Brush the entire surface with the roux. Scatter minced scallions evenly over the dough. Tightly roll the dough into a long and skinny log, as recipe tester Rachel Gascon puts it.

4 Cut crosswise into three equal pieces. Working one at a time, stretch a piece gently. Take one edge and coil it horizontally (like a snail shell). Pinch and tuck the end of the coil beneath it. Flatten the coil into a disc about 5 inches (13 cm) in diameter. It's okay if the dough rips a little or a few scallions pop out. Repeat the process with the remaining two log pieces. Cover and rest for 20 minutes.

5 *Meanwhile, make the dipping sauce.* Add all the ingredients together in a serving bowl and mix to combine. Cover and set aside.

6 Add about 2 teaspoons of neutral oil to a frying pan over medium heat. Once the oil is hot, fry the pancakes. Cook each side of the pancakes for about 3 to 4 minutes, until golden brown. Rest for a few minutes on oil-absorbing paper, slice, and enjoy!

PREP TIME	30 MINUTES
INACTIVE TIME	ABOUT 160 MINUTES
COOK TIME	25 MINUTES
YIELD	3 SCALLION PANCAKES

You can freeze leftover uncooked boba for up to 3 months.

DIY Boba Adventure

My first homemade boba was a disaster. I added too much water and made unsalvageable Newtonian fluid! Then I added less water and got a dusty, crumbly mess! Tapioca flour can be so finicky. Luckily, I've discovered two surprisingly easy ways to make boba at home. Choose either way and have a fun boba adventure!

FOR BOBA, THE FIRST WAY

About ½ to ¾ cup
(64 to 90 g) tapioca
flour, plus extra
for dusting

2 tablespoons
(30 g) packed dark
brown sugar

About ¼ cup (62 g)
silken tofu

1 tablespoon (15 g)
water

FOR BOBA, THE SECOND WAY

¼ cup (60 g) packed
dark brown sugar

1¼ cups (160 g)
tapioca flour, plus more
for dusting, divided

About ⅓ cup (78 g)
water

**FOR THE BROWN SUGAR–
WATER MIXTURE**

¾ cup (170 g) packed
dark brown sugar

1½ cups (355 g) water

FOR THE BOBA TEA

Milk of choice or milk
tea (tea with any milk)

Ice cubes (optional)

1 *Make boba, the first way.* Add the tapioca flour, dark brown sugar, tofu, and water to a medium bowl. Knead until a well-incorporated and smooth dough forms. This takes a little time and patience. Shape into a ball before rolling it into a long, thin log.

/ OR /

Make boba, the second way. In a large bowl, add the dark brown sugar, ¼ cup (32 g) tapioca flour, and water and mix until incorporated. Microwave on high power for 1 minute. Then, add the sticky dough to a stand mixer fitted with the dough hook attachment. Slowly add 1 cup (128 g) tapioca flour and mix for about 1 minute at low speed. Wear food-safe gloves. When cool enough to touch, hand knead and stretch the dough until smooth and elastic, incorporating the remaining tapioca flour. Roll it into a long, thin log.

2 *Shape and boil the boba.* In a medium bowl, spread tapioca flour and set aside. This will be used to coat the uncooked boba so they won't stick to each other.

3 Cut the boba dough log into small equal squares (about ¼ inch [6 mm] each). Round each square into a ball and drop into the prepared bowl. Roll the boba around to coat with tapioca flour. Transfer the coated boba to a fine-mesh strainer to sift off the extra tapioca flour.

4 Fill a large pot halfway with water and bring to a boil. Drop in the boba, reduce to medium heat, and cook for 15 minutes. Your boba will puff up in size as it absorbs water. Strain the boba.

5 *Make the brown sugar water mixture.* In a large pot, add the ingredients and mix. Bring to a boil, while mixing continuously, and then reduce the heat to low. Add the boba and simmer for about 15 minutes while continuously stirring.

6 Use a slotted spoon to add your desired amount of boba into serving glasses. Add ice and milk or milk tea to make boba tea!

PREP TIME	**25 MINUTES**
COOK TIME	**ABOUT 25 MINUTES**
YIELD	**BOBA FOR 4 BOBA DRINKS**

Pillowy Steamed Buns

Legend has it that *mantou*, or unfilled Chinese steamed buns, once saved the lives of at least fifty men, thanks to the quick wit of Zhuge Liang, a strategist famous in Chinese history. Zhuge Liang had steamed buns made to resemble and replace human heads that needed to be sacrificed to appease a river deity.

Although *mantou* sounds like "barbarian's head" in Chinese, fret not! These soft and fluffy vegetarian buns are not made for cannibals, and they can be made vegan if you substitute the milk with plant-based milk.

FOR THE BUN DOUGH

¾ cup plus 1 tablespoon (190 g) milk

1 teaspoon active dry yeast

Dash of sugar

About 2⅜ cups (300 g) all-purpose flour, sifted

Pinch of salt

¼ cup (50 g) granulated sugar

1 tablespoon (15 g) vegetable or canola oil

FOR THE WASH

Cream or milk

1 Microwave the milk in 15-second bursts, until it reaches about 110°F (43°C), which feels warmer than body temperature but not hot.

2 *Make the bun dough.* In a bowl, add the milk, yeast, and a dash of sugar. Stir and set aside for a few minutes. If the mixture foams and bubbles, the yeast is alive.

3 In a stand mixer fitted with the dough hook attachment (or by hand with a wooden spoon or chopsticks), tip in the flour and salt and then slowly add the milk mixture, sugar, and oil. Mix on low speed just until a smooth and elastic dough forms, a few minutes. Do not overwork the dough. Shape into a ball, cover, and let rest for 20 minutes.

4 Line two bamboo steamers with perforated steamer parchment paper. (Alternatively, cut eight 4½- x 4½-inch [11.5 x 11.5 cm] parchment paper squares and place one bun on each square before proofing.)

5 Knead the dough for a few seconds. Using a lightly floured rolling pin, roll out into a rectangle of about 14 x 8 inches (35.5 x 20.5 cm). Roll the short end into a tight log, from left to right. Cut the log into eight even 1 inch (2.5 cm) buns.*

Place four buns directly in each prepared steamer about 2 inches (5 cm) apart. The buns should be standing (with the swirls visible on both sides), not lying flat. Cover and proof for 60 minutes, until roughly doubled in size.

6 Brush cream or milk evenly over the tops of the buns.

7 With one steamer stacked on top of the other and the top steamer covered, steam the buns for about 12 to 15 minutes over high heat (see steaming technique on page 17). Periodically check the water level of the wok or pot and replenish with hot water, as needed.

8 After turning off the heat, rest the buns in the steamers for 5 minutes before removing the lid. Serve warm.

*To make gua bao buns (folded filled buns) instead, *after dividing the dough log, shape each piece into a ball and roll into a ½-inch (1.3 cm) disc. Brush the top with some neutral oil. Fold the bun in half and place it on the steamer. Repeat with the remaining seven pieces of the dough to make a total of eight bao buns. After proofing for 60 minutes, steam for about 9 minutes over high heat.*

PREP TIME	**20 MINUTES**
INACTIVE TIME	**ABOUT 80 MINUTES**
COOK TIME	**ABOUT 12 MINUTES**
YIELD	**8 BUNS**

Satisfying Korean Egg Bread

When you cut into a crispy, fluffy Korean Egg Bread (or *gyeran-ppang*), you'll feel like you're looking at the sun. Eating this egg bread, I imagine myself exploring the exhilarating and busy streets of Seoul. On days when you're time poor, I hope you'll turn to this recipe. Plus, you can quickly make Korean Egg Bread for any meal throughout the year.

This gyeran-ppang includes chia seeds in the batter for an added crunch. Feel free to add any toppings of choice, such as spinach, kimchi, cheese, or just let the baked egg be the star!

Note: Be sure to soak the chia seeds in about 5 tablespoons (75 g) of filtered water for 30 minutes before adding them to the batter. Drain the chia seeds first if there's any excess water.

RECIPE SPECS

FOR THE BATTER

About ⅔ cup (85 g) all-purpose flour

1 tablespoon (8 g) tapioca flour

¼ cup (50 g) granulated sugar

1 teaspoon baking powder

¼ teaspoon nutmeg (optional)

⅓ cup (75 g) butter, melted

1 egg (about 2 ounces, or 50 g)

⅓ cup (80 g) milk

1 tablespoon (13 g) chia seeds, soaked

1 teaspoon vanilla extract (optional)

FOR THE TOPPINGS

6 small eggs (about 9 ounces, or 228 g), uncracked

Dashes of salt, pepper, and paprika, or to taste

1 tablespoon (5 g) grated Parmesan cheese (optional)

1 teaspoon black sesame seeds (optional)

2 scallions, minced (optional)

1 Preheat the oven to 365°F (185°C, or gas mark 5) and place a rack in the center.

2 Generously grease a 6-cup muffin pan.

3 *Mix the batter.* In a large bowl, mix all the batter ingredients until smooth and combined.

4 Fill one-fourth of each muffin pan cup with the batter. Set the remaining batter aside. Crack one egg into each cup. Season the eggs with salt, pepper, and paprika. Top each egg with 1 to 2 teaspoons of the remaining batter. Optionally, top each bread with a dash of Parmesan cheese, a few sesame seeds, and some minced scallions. Be sure the cups are not overflowing.

5 Bake for about 15 minutes, until the tops are golden brown.

6 Remove from the oven. I like to enjoy these hot. Take the egg breads out of the muffin cups. Slice each in half to see the egg's lovely sun-like cross section.

Refrigerate leftover batter and use it within a few days. Bake to make plain chia muffins.

PREP TIME	**15 MINUTES**
COOK TIME	**ABOUT 15 MINUTES**
YIELD	**6 PIECES**

If you'd like a pop of green, add a handful of minced chives, parsley, or scallions to your batter.

Eggless Mochi Cheese Puffs

If French *gougères* and Brazilian *pão de queijo* had babies, their offspring would be these eggless mochi cheese puffs. What makes these puffs different from their hypothetical parents is that they're chewier and egg- and gluten-free and much easier and quicker to bake. You won't have to worry about heating milk, overcooking eggs, or making choux dough. Just worry about how quickly these addictive puffs will disappear.

This recipe is inspired by one found on SAB by Rachelle Cheng.

RECIPE SPECS

FOR THE DOUGH

1⅓ cups (160 g) glutinous rice flour

About 2 tablespoons (15 g) tapioca flour

1 teaspoon miso

1 teaspoon baking powder

1 tablespoon (14 g) butter, melted

About ½ cup plus 1 tablespoon (140 g) milk

Pinches of black pepper and salt, or to taste

Dash of paprika

About ½ cup (50 g) freshly grated Parmesan or sharp cheddar cheese

FOR THE OPTIONAL WASH

Milk

1 Preheat the oven to 365°F (185°C, or gas mark 5) and place a rack in the center. Grease a 12-cup muffin pan. (A parchment paper–lined baking sheet works too.)

2 *Make the dough.* In a stand mixer fitted with the paddle attachment, mix all the dough ingredients at medium-low speed until a dough forms, scraping down the sides of the bowl as needed. The dough should resemble firm vanilla ice cream. Add the grated cheese and mix until just incorporated. Divide the dough into eight to ten portions, about 42 g (1½ ounces) each. Apply pressure with your palms as you roll and firmly shape each piece of dough to resemble a ping pong ball.

3 Place one dough ball in each muffin pan cavity. Using a pastry brush, brush the tops with milk, if desired.

4 Bake for about 20 to 25 minutes, until the tops are golden and your kitchen smells like a pizzeria. Remove the puffs from the oven and cool directly in the muffin pan. Once cooled, the puffs may spread and deflate a bit.

To make these puffs vegan, please use vegan butter, plant-based milk, and vegan cheese.

PREP TIME	15 MINUTES
COOK TIME	20 TO 25 MINUTES
YIELD	8 TO 10 PUFFS

Dorayaki Pancakes with Anko Paste

Dorayaki, a beloved Japanese confection, has been around since the time of the samurai. Although I enjoy dorayaki the traditional way (two pretty pancakes sandwiching sweet red bean, or *anko*, paste), feel free to use different fillings, such as peanut butter and jelly or blueberry cream cheese. You could even sandwich a purin (page 148) perfectly between these pancakes!

Note: To make the anko paste, you'll have to soak the red beans overnight and then boil them for over an hour.

This recipe is adapted from one found on justonecookbook.com by the illustrious Namiko (Nami) Hirasawa Chen, whom SAB members and I adore.

FOR THE ANKO PASTE

1 cup (197 g) dried
red beans

¾ cup (150 g)
granulated sugar

1 teaspoon miso

1 teaspoon lemon
juice (optional)

1 teaspoon lemon
zest (optional)

FOR THE PANCAKE BATTER

4 medium eggs (about
7 ounces, or 200 g)

⅓ cup (67 g)
granulated sugar

1 tablespoon (15 g) milk

1 teaspoon vanilla
extract (optional)

1 cup (125 g)
all-purpose flour

1 teaspoon baking
powder

½ teaspoon salt

1 *Make the anko paste.* Soak the red beans overnight. Drain and place in a pot with at least 2 inches (5 cm) of water over the beans. Boil over high heat for about 1 minute. Discard the water and add fresh water to the pot, again at least 2 inches (5 cm) above the beans. Boil the water again over high heat. Once the water is boiling, reduce the heat to medium-low. Simmer the beans until tender, about 70 minutes. Occasionally check to see whether you need to replenish the water in the pot.

2 Once the beans are soft, drain them. Using a fork or wooden spoon, mash the beans and combine with the sugar, miso, and optional lemon juice and zest in a bowl. Set aside.

3 Dampen a clean, lint-free kitchen towel.

4 *Make the pancake batter.* In a large bowl, whisk the eggs, sugar, milk, and vanilla extract together until well incorporated. Sift in the flour, baking powder, and salt and whisk until smooth and homogeneous. Cover and chill for 30 minutes.

5 Brush a neutral oil over a frying pan and then wipe it off. Heat the pan over medium-low heat for 1 to 2 minutes. Then, reduce the heat to low. Using a ladle or a small measuring cup, pour 3 tablespoons (about 45 to 50 g) of batter into the center of the pan. The pancake should be about 3 inches (7.5 cm) in diameter. Cook for about 2 minutes, until bubbles form. Like with all other pancakes, that's when you flip it.

6 Cook the second side of the pancake for about 1 minute, until dark golden brown. Transfer to a plate and cover with the damp towel. Repeat to make nine to eleven more pancakes.

7 *Assemble the dorayaki.* Sandwich 2 tablespoons (about 30 g) of the anko paste between two pancakes. Use the nicer-looking side of each pancake as the outside of the sandwich.

Dorayaki pancakes are usually made with honey. If you'd like a sweeter pancake, try adding 1 to 2 teaspoons of honey to the pancake batter, or about 1 teaspoon of mirin, a sweet Japanese cooking wine.

PREP TIME	**20 MINUTES**
INACTIVE TIME	**OVERNIGHT (IF MAKING THE ANKO PASTE)**
COOK TIME	**100 TO 120 MINUTES (IF MAKING THE ANKO PASTE)**
YIELD	**5 TO 6 ASSEMBLED PANCAKES**

Tanghulu Candied Fruits

Since the Song Dynasty, people have been enjoying *tanghulu* or *bingtanghulu*. Bingtanghulu's literal translation is "ice sugar bottle gourd." One bite and the sugar shell snaps like thin ice, revealing a soft, juicy fruit.

Notes: If you don't have a candy thermometer, test the temperature of the sugar syrup by dipping a spoon into ice water. Wipe off the water and dip the spoon into the syrup. If the syrup hardens immediately on the spoon, then you've reached the right temperature to coat fruits. Traditionally, tanghulu fruits have a thicker sugar coating than pictured. For a thicker, glass-like coating, roll the fruit in the bubbling syrup a few times instead of just dipping it in the syrup. You'll need ten to twelve bamboo skewers for this recipe.

About 1½ cups (220 g) fruit, such as strawberries, grapes, blueberries, or peeled tangerines, washed and dried (with skins intact and not sliced)

1½ cups (300 g) granulated sugar

About ⅔ cup (150 g) water

1 teaspoon vanilla extract (optional)

1 Line a baking sheet with parchment paper.

2 Skewer the fruits. Add about three pieces of fruit to each bamboo skewer if using grapes or blueberries and one piece to each skewer if using peeled tangerines or strawberries.

3 In a saucepan, heat the sugar and water over medium heat until it reaches 300°F (150°C). Reaching the proper temperature takes about 10 minutes or longer. When ready, the sugar syrup should be amber-colored and a little thicker.

4 Reduce the heat to low and quickly and carefully coat the fruits with the hot sugar syrup. *Do not hold* the skewers upright immediately after coating the fruits. The hot syrup can drip from the fruits and burn your hands. (It has happened to me!) Transfer the tanghulu skewers to the prepared baking sheet, laying them flat. Once the sugar coating hardens, and that'll be relatively quickly, serve and enjoy!

5 Tanghulu fruits can be wrapped in plastic wrapping and stored in the refrigerator for about 3 days or in the freezer for up to 1 month.

PREP TIME	10 MINUTES
COOK TIME	10 TO 15 MINUTES
YIELD	10 TO 12 SKEWERS, DEPENDING ON THE FRUITS USED

Substitute the milk or buttermilk powder with matcha for green, matcha-flavored crisps, shown on page 45. You can do the same with cocoa powder for cocoa-flavored crisps. Feel free to change up your mix-ins.

Chewy Taiwanese Snowflake Crisps

Confession time! This is my favorite recipe in the entire book. Why? Well firstly, it's super versatile and easy to make. Secondly, I'm simply addicted to snowflake crisps (or nougat cracker candy). I've finished entire bags on my own. (Don't judge!) Each bite is an addictive harmony of *yin* and *yang:* chewy yet crispy, sweet yet salty, and milky yet light.

It's no wonder this confection is one of the best-selling snacks across Taiwan and Hong Kong, and it's a social media star.

RECIPE SPECS

¼ cup (½ stick, or 55 g) salted or unsalted butter

About 3½ cups (180 g) mini white or colored marshmallows (or cut-up large ones)

1 tablespoon (15 g) milk powder or buttermilk powder, plus more for dusting

1 teaspoon vanilla extract

About 40 buttery salted snack crackers (130 g)

About ½ cup (76 g) salted nuts of choice, chopped (such as salted pistachios)

About ½ cup (70 g) dried fruits of choice (such as cranberries or raisins)

1 Generously grease or line an 8- x 8-inch (20.5 x 20.5 cm) baking pan with parchment paper.

2 In a large saucepan, melt the butter over medium heat. Reduce the heat to medium-low and add the marshmallows. Stir continuously until all the marshmallow melts, resembling melty mozzarella cheese. (Alternatively, you can melt the butter and marshmallows in the microwave, in 20-second bursts, stirring after each burst.)

3 Add the milk powder (or buttermilk powder) and vanilla extract and stir until incorporated. Add the crackers, nuts, and dried fruits.

4 Using a flexible spatula or wooden spoon, stir until everything is well coated with the marshmallow-butter mixture. The crackers, nuts, and fruits should be spread evenly so each bite will have a little of everything. At this point, it's up to you whether to crush and break up the crackers. I prefer the crackers a bit more intact. Remove from heat.

5 Transfer the mixture to the prepared pan. Wear a pair of greased food-safe gloves. When the mixture is cool to the touch, pull, stretch, and knead it a little, using your hands. Evenly press the mixture into the coated pan using your hands (or a greased spatula). You want the mixture to be about ½ to ¾ inch (1.3 to 2 cm) thick and leveled, so don't overflatten it. Cover and let rest on the counter for 30 minutes.

6 Cut into 12 to 16 even pieces. Dust all over with milk powder. Enjoy one (or two) and then hide or share the rest of these tempting bites. Store in an airtight container and eat within a few days.

PREP TIME	10 MINUTES
INACTIVE TIME	ABOUT 60 MINUTES
COOK TIME	10 MINUTES
YIELD	12 TO 16 CRISPS

Velvety Nama Chocolates

Before I leave Narita Airport on my return trips from Japan, I always stock up on Royce's famous *nama* chocolates. These confections are the epitome of perfect velvety chocolate truffles. I love biting into a soft nama chocolate and letting the ganache melt on my tongue. I'm a sucker for anything comforting and delicious yet simply made.

This recipe is inspired by Royce's nama chocolates.

Notes: *Nama* means raw or fresh in Japanese, and nama chocolates are easily made with fresh cream and chocolate. Please have a digital or candy thermometer for this recipe.

RECIPE SPECS

FOR THE NAMA CHOCOLATES

1 cup (235 g) heavy cream

1 tablespoon (14 g) butter

About 2 cups (470 g) bittersweet or dark couverture (or high quality) chocolate, chopped

1 tablespoon (15 g) liquor of choice or vanilla extract (optional)

A pinch of salt

Cocoa powder for dusting

Gold flakes for garnishing (optional)

FOR THE MATCHA NAMA

1 cup (235 g) heavy cream

2 tablespoons (28 g) butter, room temperature

About 3 cups (470 g) ivory-colored white chocolate (made with cocoa butter), chopped

1 teaspoon vanilla extract

Pinch of salt

1 to 2 tablespoons (6 to 12 g) matcha, plus more for dusting

Edible gold flakes or sea salt flakes for garnishing (optional)

1 Line an 8 x 8-inch (20.5 x 20.5 cm) baking pan with parchment paper.

2 *Make the nama chocolates.* In a saucepan, heat the heavy cream and butter to 120°F (49°C). Remove from heat. Add the chocolate to a large heatproof bowl and microwave for 15 seconds. Pour the cream into the softened chocolates to temper them. Add the optional liquor or vanilla extract and a pinch of salt. Whisk until creamy and homogeneous. Refer to the *final step.*

/ OR /

Make matcha nama chocolates. In a saucepan, heat the heavy cream and butter to 110°F (43°C), until the butter has melted. Immediately remove from heat and mix in the white chocolate, vanilla extract, and salt until incorporated and creamy. Sift in the matcha and whisk until homogeneous.

3 *The final step:* Pour the chocolate mixture into the prepared pan. Even and smooth out the top of the chocolate. Tap the pan against the counter to get rid of air bubbles. Cover with plastic wrap and refrigerate for at least 3 hours.

4 Depending on how big you want the nama chocolates to be, you can slice the chocolate into twenty-four to thirty-six equal pieces. Dust with either the cocoa or matcha. Feel free to garnish with edible gold flakes or sea salt flakes.

5 Nama chocolates should be refrigerated in an airtight container and eaten within 5 days.

Take care not to overheat the heavy cream or the chocolate will separate. To enjoy nama chocolates in a different way, try wrapping them with a mochi dough disc (page 24).

PREP TIME	15 MINUTES
COOK TIME	10 MINUTES
YIELD	24 TO 36 PIECES

Kawaii (cute) alert! Reserve a bit of dough from each color to make animal ears. Wet the dango a little before sticking on the ears. You can also shape the dango dough into hearts or other shapes before boiling them. Draw cute faces on the cooled dango by piping melted chocolate or using toothpicks dipped in chocolate.

Hanami Dango with Sweet Soy Sauce Glaze

As early as the eighth century, the Japanese would make and eat *hanami dango* to welcome spring. *Hanami* means "flower viewing" and *dango* means "dumpling." The pink dango symbolizes the arrival of *sakura* (or cherry blossoms) while the white in the middle represents either white cherry blossom flowers or snow.

The green dango (leaves) is traditionally made with mugwort. I haven't worked with mugwort yet, so we'll use matcha instead.

Note: Please have six bamboo skewers handy.

RECIPE SPECS

FOR THE DANGO

About ¾ cup plus 1 tablespoon (100 g) glutinous rice flour

¼ cup (30 g) confectioners' sugar

About ½ cup (110 g) silken tofu

¼ teaspoon vanilla extract (optional)

¼ teaspoon matcha

1 teaspoon red beet powder or strawberry powder

A drop of red food coloring gel (optional)

FOR THE OPTIONAL MITARASHI (SWEET SOY SAUCE) GLAZE

1 tablespoon (15 g) soy sauce

1 tablespoon (8 g) cornstarch

2 tablespoons (30 g) packed brown sugar, adjust to taste

1 tablespoon (15 g) mirin or (20 g) honey

2 tablespoons (30 g) water

1 *Make the dango.* In a large bowl, combine the glutinous rice flour, sugar, tofu, and optional vanilla extract. Knead until a smooth, claylike dough forms. The dough should be a little shiny and feel like an earlobe, as the Japanese say. If the dough is too wet, dust with a little glutinous rice flour, and if it's too dry, add a little more tofu.

2 Divide the dough into three equal portions.

3 In a medium bowl, add the matcha. Transfer one piece of dough into the bowl and knead until uniformly green. In another bowl, add the red beet or strawberry powder, transfer another piece of dough into this bowl, and knead until uniformly pink. Mix in a drop of red food coloring to enhance the color.

4 The final piece of dough will be off-white.

5 Divide each of the three dough portions into six balls weighing approximately ⅓ ounce (10 g) each, making a total of eighteen balls (for six bamboo skewers). Transfer the balls into a large pot of boiling water and cook for about 4 minutes, until they float.

6 Fill a large bowl with ice and water. Remove the dango with a slotted spoon or a mesh skimmer and transfer them into the ice water for about 30 seconds.

7 To assemble the hanami dango skewers, first add a green, then a white, and finally a pink dango to each one. Place your completed skewers on a serving plate.

8 *Make the optional mitarashi glaze.* In a small saucepan, add all the ingredients and whisk until combined. Cook over low heat, stirring continuously until the sauce thickens and can coat the back of a spoon. Drizzle over the dango.

PREP TIME	25 MINUTES
COOK TIME	ABOUT 3 MINUTES TO COOK THE DANGO
YIELD	6 COMPLETED SKEWERS WITH 3 DANGO EACH

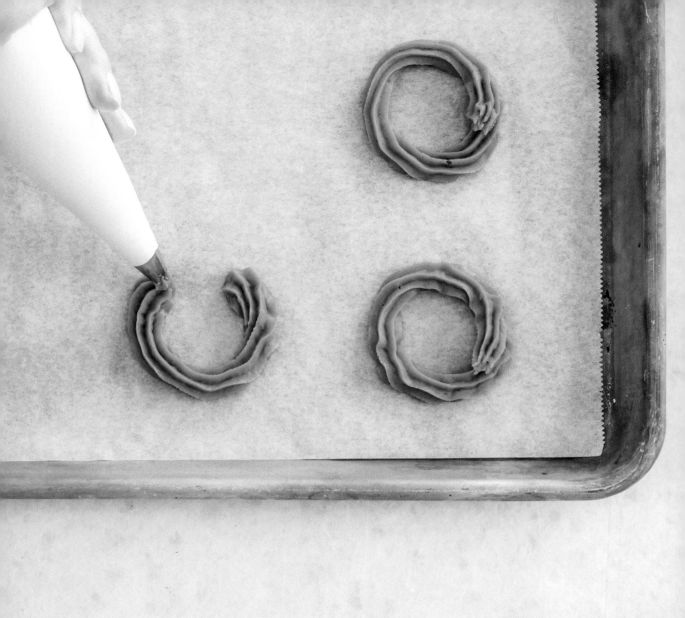

SAB's Favorite Cookies and Pastries

In 2020, my good friend Will Leung hosted a live cookie bake-along on SAB, teaching members how to make delicious matcha and white chocolate chip cookies. It was the first time I made cookies from scratch, and I instantly fell in love with the process.

Cookie dough tends to be forgiving, as long as it's not overmixed. To start with something easy, try my Butterfly Pea Flower Shortbread recipe (page 64). We'll use a standard 1 part sugar, 2 parts fat, 3 parts flour "shortbread ratio" to make buttery and beautifully blue, modern-looking cookies, baked into any shape you desire. They're perfect as a snack or as part of a cookie tin for gifting.

Another cookie that's perfect as a gift are the moon-sized Black Sesame Neapolitan Sugar Cookies (page 56). They're tri-colored and fancy and made with three delicious Asian flavors. Feel free to experiment and change up the flavors to make the cookies your own.

You'll also find some of my favorite pastry recipes in this section. Many of them are QQ-chewy and made with mochi, such as my gorgeous and vibrant Ube Butter Mochi (page 54), Black Sesame Mochi Beignets (page 68), and Mochi *Pon de Ring* Donuts (page 66).

I hope you'll have fun with these recipes and love them as much as the SAB Community and I do.

Monstrous Matcha Miso Cookies

I'm obsessed with these enormous cakey verdant cookies. They're not too sweet (yay!) and full of umami, thanks to the addition of matcha and miso. As they're monstrous in size, I recommend you only eat one at a time. (But if you must have more, I wouldn't judge!)

Whenever I bake a batch of these green monsters, I share them with my neighbor and SAB member, Kelley Bravo. I dedicate this recipe to you, Kelley!

The world-famous Levain Bakery cookies from New York City inspired this recipe.

RECIPE SPECS

About 1½ cups (180 g) all-purpose flour

About 1⅓ cups (180 g) cake flour

½ teaspoon baking powder

½ teaspoon baking soda

1 teaspoon cornstarch

1 to 2 tablespoons (6 to 12 g) matcha, adjust to taste

1 cup (2 sticks, or 225 g) butter, room temperature, cut into cubes

¾ cup (170 g) packed brown sugar

¼ cup (50 g) granulated sugar

2 medium eggs (about 3½ ounces, or 100 g), room temperature

1 tablespoon (16 g) miso or ½ teaspoon salt

1½ to 2 cups (360 to 480 g) bittersweet or semisweet chocolate (chips or chunks)

About ½ cup (85 g) nuts of choice (optional)

1 Preheat the oven to 400°F (200°C, or gas mark 6) and place a rack in the center. Line two large baking sheets with parchment paper.

2 In a bowl, sift in the flours, baking powder, baking soda, cornstarch, matcha, and ½ teaspoon of salt if not using the miso. Set aside.

3 In a stand mixer fitted with the paddle attachment, beat the butter and sugars on medium-high speed until light and fluffy, a few minutes. Add the eggs and miso (if using). Mix on low speed until combined and smooth, scraping down the sides of the bowl as needed to incorporate the ingredients.

4 Tip in the bowl of dry ingredients. Mix until a cookiedough forms. Fold the chocolate chips (or chunks) and optional nuts into the cookie dough.

5 Drop about four heaping scoops of dough onto a baking sheet, spaced at least 2 inches (5 cm) apart. Flattening the dough balls, which is optional, will produce smoothly textured cookies, as shown. Skip this step for chunkier and more textured cookies. (You can freeze them, uncovered, for about 30 minutes. Just be sure to increase the baking time by a few minutes if you do.)

6 Bake for about 15 minutes, until the tops are golden and the edges begin to darken. As these are *thick* cookies, the centers will be soft and the melted chocolate will be gooey.

7 Remove from the oven. Cool directly on the baking sheets to allow the cookies to set. The cookie centers should be soft and gooey but not runny. Enjoy!

8 Store leftover cookies in an airtight container and consume within a few days. Reheat in the toaster or oven at 350°F (180°C, or gas mark 4) for a few minutes.

PREP TIME	20 MINUTES
COOK TIME	ABOUT 15 MINUTES
YIELD	8 LARGE COOKIES

If you don't have ube halaya jam handy, replace it with ½ to 1 tablespoon (8 to 15 g) of ube extract and add one more egg to the batter.

Ube Butter Mochi

When Regina Ramirez (my neighbor and SAB member) posted a gorgeous picture of her ube butter mochi on SAB, I grabbed a kitchen towel to wipe away my drool. Regina's butter mochi bites were spectacular: gloriously purple, shiny, and super crave-worthy. You could imagine how deliciously buttery and chewy they were! I was obsessed and had to make my own batch of beautiful ube butter mochi.

This recipe is inspired by Regina and adapted from one found on keepingitrelle.com.

Note: Macapuno strings are fleshy shredded coconut typically used in Filipino desserts. They are usually preserved, bottled in syrup, and easily found in Asian supermarkets.

RECIPE SPECS

About ½ cup (160 g) homemade ube halaya jam (see page 28), or store-bought

3 medium eggs (about 5 ounces, or 150 g)

About 2 cups (470 g) milk or evaporated milk

1 14-ounce (400 g) can coconut milk

1 teaspoon vanilla extract

1 teaspoon ube extract

½ cup (1 stick, or 112 g) butter, melted

1 tablespoon (16 g) miso

¼ cup (68 g) macapuno-sweetened coconut strings (optional)

3⅓ cups (400 g) glutinous rice flour

1¼ cups (250 g) granulated sugar

2 teaspoons baking powder

Toasted coconut flakes for topping (optional)

1 Generously grease or line (including the sides) a 9 x 13-inch (23 x 33 cm) baking pan with parchment paper.

2 Preheat the oven to 350°F (180°C, or gas mark 4) and place a rack in the center.

3 In a stand mixer fitted with the paddle attachment, add the ube jam, eggs, milk, coconut milk, vanilla extract, ube extract, melted butter, miso, and optional coconut strings. Mix on low speed until well incorporated, scraping down the sides of the bowl as needed. Sift in the glutinous rice flour, sugar, and baking powder. Mix on low speed until the batter is smooth and thoroughly combined. Again, scrape down the sides of the bowl as needed to incorporate the ingredients. Cover and let rest for 20 minutes.

4 Pour the mixture into the prepared pan. Tap the pan against your counter to release any air bubbles.

5 Bake for about 60 to 70 minutes, until the top is golden brown and the butter mochi is set. Turn off the oven and leave the butter mochi inside for about 15 minutes, until a nice golden and crispy crust develops. Remove from the oven and allow to cool completely before cutting into twelve to sixteen even pieces.

6 Top with the optional toasted coconut flakes and enjoy!

While most people may say butter mochi is best eaten the day they're made, I enjoy them a day or two after when they've aged and developed more of a chew. Store leftover butter mochi in an airtight container at room temperature for up to two days. Refrigerated butter mochi can be revived in a toaster or oven.

PREP TIME	10 MINUTES
COOK TIME	ABOUT 70 MINUTES
YIELD	12 TO 16 PIECES, DEPENDING ON THE SIZE

For different flavors, try grinding tea leaves, such as oolong, earl grey, or *hojicha* (green tea), into a fine powder to substitute any of the powders used in this recipe.

Black Sesame Neapolitan Sugar Cookies

Three gorgeous colors, crispy edges, and a tender center make these Asian-style Neapolitan cookies irresistible. They'll stay soft for days, so while tempting, there's no need to eat them all in one sitting! Definitely share these beautiful cookies and impress your friends and loved ones.

This recipe was inspired by one found on SAB by Andrea Chen (@ispillice on Instagram), who adapted a recipe found on constellationinspiration.com.

RECIPE SPECS

1 cup (2 sticks, or 225 g) butter, room temperature

¾ cup (150 g) granulated sugar

¼ cup (60 g) packed brown sugar

1 egg (about 2 ounces, or 50 g), room temperature, beaten

1 teaspoon vanilla extract

1 tablespoon (16 g) miso

2 cups (250 g) all-purpose flour

½ teaspoon baking powder

½ teaspoon baking soda

3 tablespoons (45 g) black sesame powder

1 to 2 tablespoons (6 to 12 g) matcha, adjust to taste

2 to 3 tablespoons (24 to 36 g) purple sweet potato powder

½ teaspoon lemon zest

Sugar for rolling the cookies (optional)

1 In a stand mixer fitted with the paddle attachment, beat the butter and sugars on medium-high speed until light and fluffy, about 3 minutes. Add the egg, vanilla extract, and miso and mix to incorporate. Stop the mixer to scrape down the sides of the bowl as needed to fully incorporate the ingredients. Add the flour, baking powder, and baking soda and mix on low speed until combined.

2 Divide the dough into three equal portions (about 235 g, or 8 ounces, each), placing each portion in a separate bowl. Add the black sesame powder to the first bowl, the matcha to the second bowl, and the purple sweet potato powder and lemon zest to the third bowl. Mix each piece of dough until each of the powders and zest are incorporated, but don't overmix. Wrap each piece of dough in plastic wrap and refrigerate for 20 minutes.

3 Preheat the oven to 350°F (180°C, or gas mark 4) with a rack in the center. Line two large baking sheets with parchment paper.

4 Spoon 1 tablespoon (about 15 g) of each dough. Combine the three pieces of dough into one dough ball by rolling them together. Repeat until you have ten to twelve large, tri-colored dough balls. Optionally, toss each ball in a bowl filled with sugar (granulated, coarse, or demerara) and coat evenly.

5 Place five to six dough balls on each prepared baking sheet, with ample spacing for each cookie to account for spreading. (They can spread dramatically.) Slightly flatten each dough ball with your palm.

6 Bake for about 15 minutes, until golden brown around the edges with soft centers.

7 Cool on the baking sheets to allow the cookies to set.

PREP TIME	25 MINUTES
COOK TIME	15 MINUTES
YIELD	10 TO 12 COOKIES, DEPENDING ON THE SIZE

Replace the berry jam with ube halaya jam (page 28) to make ube matcha cream bars. Pistachios in the short-bread can be replaced with raw pine nuts.

Berry Matcha Cream Bars

One bite of these dreamy creamy bars and I'm transported to Shinjuku Gyoen National Garden in Tokyo during the springtime when sakura are in full bloom. This berry cream layer atop a buttery and earthy shortbread combo is, without a doubt, a *matcha* made in heaven.

This recipe is adapted from one found on SAB by Hali Mo (@halicopteraway on Instagram).

FOR THE MATCHA SHORTBREAD

¾ cup (1½ sicks, or 165 g) butter, softened

¼ cup (50 g) granulated sugar

1 teaspoon miso

About 1½ cups (180 g) all-purpose flour, sifted

1 tablespoon (6 g) matcha

About ¼ cup (35 g) pistachios, finely chopped

FOR THE BERRY CREAM

¼ cup (60 g) water

2¼ teaspoons powdered gelatin (one standard packet)

About 2 cups (470 g) full-fat coconut milk

2 tablespoons (40 g) condensed milk or honey, adjust to taste

½ teaspoon miso

4 tablespoons (80 g) raspberry or strawberry jam

1 teaspoon lemon zest or lemon juice

1 drop red food coloring gel (optional)

⅓ cup (40 g) dried cranberries (optional)

FOR THE OPTIONAL TOPPINGS

Matcha or strawberry powder

Fresh raspberries or sliced strawberries

Edible gold flakes

1 *Make the matcha shortbread.* Preheat the oven to 350°F (180°C, or gas mark 4) and place a rack in the center.

2 Grease or line a 9 x 9-inch (23 x 23 cm) baking pan with parchment paper.

3 In a stand mixer fitted with the paddle attachment, beat the butter, sugar, and miso until well incorporated and fluffy, about 2 minutes. Scrape down the sides of the bowl as needed. Add the flour and matcha and mix on medium-low speed until a dough forms. Fold the pistachios into the dough until evenly distributed.

4 Transfer the shortbread dough to the prepared pan. Using the back of a spoon or clean fingers, firmly press the mixture evenly over the bottom of the pan, covering all edges and the sides. Use a fork to poke holes across the entire surface of the dough.

5 Bake for 15 minutes, until lightly browned and puffy. Remove from the oven and cool for 10 minutes. Cover and refrigerate for 30 minutes.

6 *Meanwhile, make the berry cream.* In a bowl, add the water and gelatin. Let the gelatin bloom (absorb water) for a few minutes and then microwave for 10 seconds, until melted.

7 In a large bowl, add the coconut milk, condensed milk or honey, miso, jam, lemon juice or zest, and optional food coloring and whisk until homogeneous. Stir in the melted gelatin and mix until combined. Fold the optional dried cranberries into the mixture. Take the pan out of the refrigerator. Pour the berry cream on top of the shortbread. Tap gently against the counter and smooth out the top with a spatula.

8 Cover and refrigerate for at least 4 hours or overnight.

9 Cut into twelve to sixteen even pieces. Garnish with the optional toppings. Enjoy! Refrigerate leftovers and consume within a few days.

PREP TIME	15 MINUTES
INACTIVE TIME	30 MINUTES
COOK TIME	15 MINUTES
YIELD	12 TO 16 BARS

Assign the "uglier" macaron shells as the bottoms of the macaron.

Lemony Matcha Macarons

When I first started baking, I was obsessed with perfecting macarons. I had little success until SAB member Rebekah Yau introduced me to the Swiss Meringue Method. It turns out that heating egg whites along with sugar results in more stable, more foolproof macarons!

Here we pair herbaceous matcha shells with citrusy buttercream.

FOR THE MACARON SHELLS

2½ to 3 egg whites (about 3 ounces, or 80 g), room temperature

¼ cup plus 1 tablespoon (63 g) granulated sugar

¼ teaspoon lemon juice

¾ cup plus 2 tablespoons (90 g) almond flour, sifted

¾ cup (90 g) confectioners' sugar, sifted

2 teaspoons matcha

Pinch of salt

FOR THE BUTTERCREAM FILLING

½ cup (1 stick, or 112 g) butter, softened and cubed

1¼ cups (150 g) confectioners' sugar

½ teaspoon lemon or yuzu juice

½ teaspoon vanilla extract

1 teaspoon lemon or yuzu zest, plus more for garnishing

1 teaspoon miso or a pinch of salt

PREP TIME	15 MINUTES
COOK TIME	25 MINUTES
YIELD	ABOUT 16 TO 19 MACARONS

1 Line a large baking sheet with parchment paper.

2 *Make the macaron shells.* Using a double boiler, heat the egg whites and sugar until the mixture reaches 122°F (50°C) and no higher to avoid cooking the egg whites. Transfer the mixture to a stand mixer fitted with a whisk attachment. Add the lemon juice and beat on medium-high speed until stiff peaks form.

3 Tip in the almond flour, confectioners' sugar, matcha, and salt and fit the stand mixer with the paddle attachment. Mix on low speed for a few seconds. Using a flexible spatula, scrape the sides of the bowl and hand mix the batter until shiny and flowy like molten lava. (As you gently swirl the batter, it should fold and sink into itself like wet sand ribbons. When you lift the batter with a spatula, you should be able to draw a continuous figure *8* with it.)

4 Fill a piping bag with the batter and pipe 1½-inch (4 cm) circles onto the prepared baking sheet. Tap the sheet against the counter five times to get rid of air bubbles. Use a toothpick to pop any visible air bubbles and smooth out the tops of the shells. Rest until a skin forms on top and the shells are no longer wet to the touch, about 30 to 60 minutes.

5 About 25 minutes before baking, preheat the oven to 325°F (170°C, or gas mark 3) and place a rack in the center. If your oven tends to run hot, try a lower temperature, such as 300°F to 315°F (150°C to 157°C, or gas mark 2).

6 *Make the buttercream filling.* Beat the butter and confectioners' sugar on medium-high speed until light and fluffy, a few minutes. Add the remaining filling ingredients and beat until combined. Transfer to a piping bag. Refrigerate or set aside.

7 Bake the macaron shells for 13 to 16 minutes, until the macaron shells peel away from the parchment paper when lifted. Cool completely.

8 Pipe the buttercream filling onto the bottom side of a shell. (I like to add some fresh lemon zest on top of the buttercream.) Sandwich together with a similarly sized macaron shell. Tada!

9 Refrigerate the macarons in an airtight container and consume within 5 days.

If the macaron shells are wrinkly, the batter was overmixed or too oily, according to SAB's resident queen of macarons, Salinda Ngo (@macanomnom on Instagram).

Gooey Fudgy Miso Brownies

My boys (and by boys, I mean my son and my husband) love brownies. I, on the other hand, have always had a love-hate relationship with them (the brownies, not my son and husband). I'll crave a brownie and then bite into one and find it too achingly sweet, rich, and filling. If only brownies could be lighter, yet still ooze with chocolate!

These gluten-free, gooey, fudgy miso brownies are the answer. They're decadent yet a bit lighter and chewier than your typical brownies. Plus, the balancing miso adds layers of depth and umami.

½ cup (1 stick, or 112 g) butter, softened

1 cup (200 g) granulated sugar

2 medium eggs (about 3½ ounces, or 100 g)

1 tablespoon (16 g) miso, or to taste

1 teaspoon vanilla extract

8 ounces (228 g) high-quality semisweet chocolate, chopped

½ cup (120 g) milk

1 cup (120 g) glutinous rice flour

¼ cup (20 g) Dutch-processed cocoa powder

1 Preheat the oven to 350°F (180°C, or gas mark 4) and place a rack in the center.

2 Line an 8 inch (20.5 cm)-square baking pan with parchment paper.

3 In a stand mixer fitted with the paddle attachment, beat the butter and sugar until well incorporated. Add the eggs, miso, and vanilla extract and mix until well combined, scraping the sides of the bowl as needed. It's okay if the mixture looks oily and gritty at this point.

4 Melt half of the chocolate with a double boiler or in the microwave in 20-second bursts. Set the other half of the chocolate aside.

5 Add the melted chocolate and milk to the stand mixer and mix on low speed until incorporated. Sift in the flour and cocoa powder. Using a flexible spatula, fold to combine. Do not overmix the brownie mixture. Fold the remaining chocolate chunks into the batter.

6 Transfer the batter to the prepared baking pan. Be sure to spread the brownie mixture evenly, covering every corner of the pan. Bake for about 50 to 60 minutes, until an inserted toothpick (or bamboo stick) comes out clean.

7 Cool completely at room temperature. Slice into nine even pieces.

8 Store leftover brownies in an airtight container and consume within a few days.

To change the flavor of your mochi brownies, try adding a tablespoon of tahini (15 g) or nut butter (16 g) of choice to the batter to add a hint of nuttiness.

PREP TIME	**15 MINUTES**
COOK TIME	**ABOUT 60 MINUTES**
YIELD	**9 BROWNIES**

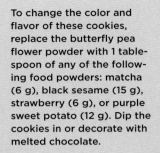

To change the color and flavor of these cookies, replace the butterfly pea flower powder with 1 tablespoon of any of the following food powders: matcha (6 g), black sesame (15 g), strawberry (6 g), or purple sweet potato (12 g). Dip the cookies in or decorate with melted chocolate.

Butterfly Pea Flower Shortbread

Butterfly pea flower, also known as Asian pigeon wings, is a common flower across Southeast Asia. When used in baking, this beautiful blue flower adds a subtle floral and nutty note to your creations. Here we'll add butterfly pea flower powder to a classic shortbread dough and make gorgeously blue, melt-in-your-mouth, buttery, and zesty cookies.

Oh and guess what? These cookies are also magical! Try adding a teaspoon of lemon juice to the cookie dough and watch as the dough transforms from blue to a gorgeous violet.

RECIPE SPECS

½ cup (1 stick, or 112 g) butter, softened

⅓ cup (67 g) granulated sugar

½ teaspoon miso

1 teaspoon lemon zest, plus more for garnishing

1 teaspoon vanilla extract

About 1⅓ cups (160 g) all-purpose flour

½ to 1 tablespoon (6 to 12 g) butterfly pea flower powder

About ¼ cup (34 g) dried cranberries, finely chopped (optional)

1 In a stand mixer fitted with the paddle attachment, cream the butter, sugar, miso, lemon zest, and vanilla extract until light and fluffy, a few minutes. Scrape down the sides of the bowl as needed. Sift in the flour and butterfly pea flower powder and mix just until just combined. It should resemble wet blue sand. Fold in the optional dried cranberries. Do not overwork the dough. Place it on top of a large sheet of plastic wrap or parchment paper.

2 Using a rolling pin, roll it into a ¼-inch to ½-inch (0.6 to 1.3 cm) rectangle (depending on how thick you like your shortbread cookies), cover, and refrigerate for 60 minutes.

3 About 30 minutes before baking, preheat the oven to 350°F (180°C, or gas mark 4) and place a rack in the center. Line a large baking sheet with parchment paper.

4 Using cookie cutters or a sharp knife, cut the dough into your desired cookie shapes. Transfer to the prepared baking sheet. Bake for 10 to 15 minutes, until the edges begin to darken. Cool for 10 minutes on the baking sheet before transferring to a wire rack to cool completely. Garnish with lemon zest.

Hannah Park, SAB member and one of my recipe testers, recommends trying this to add textural and visual contrast to the outside of the cookies: Roll the dough into a log, refrigerate, then brush the entire outside of the log with water or milk. Roll and coat the log in granulated or demerara sugar. Cut the log into ¼- to ½-inch (0.6 to 1.3 cm) pieces.

PREP TIME	10 MINUTES
COOK TIME	10 TO 15 MINUTES
YIELD	10 TO 12 COOKIES

If you find piping Pon de Rings too time consuming or challenging, feel free to pipe 3-inch (7.5 cm) O-shape donuts instead.

Mochi Pon de Ring Donuts

Mochi donuts are known for being delightfully crispy and QQ-chewy at the same time. Here we combine a semi-cooked mochi dough with uncooked ingredients to create a smooth, pipeable dough-batter that will hold its shape.

This recipe is inspired by Mister Donut's Pon de Ring donuts in Japan.

The idea to mix the donut dough on high speed came from watching many videos on how bakeries mass-produce their mochi donuts in commercial mixers. Their dough always looks elastic and fluffy, like butter slime.

FOR THE STICKY COOKED DOUGH

About ½ cup plus 2 tablespoons (72 g) glutinous rice flour

About 6 tablespoons (106 g) milk, boiling

FOR THE DONUT DOUGH

About ½ cup plus 2 tablespoons (72 g) glutinous rice flour

About 2 tablespoons (16 g) bread flour

1 tablespoon (8 g) tapioca flour

2½ tablespoons (50 g) honey

1 egg (about 2 ounces, or 50 g)

Pinch of salt

2 teaspoons baking powder

½ tablespoon (8 g) oil or (7 g) melted butter

FOR THE STRAWBERRY GLAZE

1 to 2 cups (120 to 240 g) confectioners' sugar, sifted

1 tablespoon (14 g) unsalted or salted butter, melted

About ⅓ cup (50 g) fresh strawberries, blended into a purée

1 Cut eight 4½ x 4½-inch (11.5 x 11.5 cm) parchment paper squares.

2 *Make the sticky cooked dough.* In a stand mixer fitted with the paddle attachment, add the glutinous rice flour and boiling milk. Mix on medium speed for 1 to 2 minutes, until a cohesive, sticky dough forms. Scrape down the sides of the mixer bowl as needed. Cover and set aside for 10 minutes.

3 *Make the donut dough.* Add all the donut dough ingredients to the stand mixer with the sticky cooked dough. Mix on medium-high speed for 2 minutes, scraping down the sides of the bowl as needed. Turn the speed up to high and mix for 1 minute. The batter should be tacky, sticky, and pipeable, somewhat like choux dough.

4 Transfer the mixture to a piping bag with a ½-inch (1.3 cm) plain round tip. Pipe eight 1 teaspoon (about 5 g) balls that connect in a ring shape (like a bead bracelet) directly on a parchment paper square. The Pon de Ring should be about 3 inches (7.5 cm) in diameter. Repeat until you make about eight Pon de Ring donuts. Wet your fingers and smooth out the tops of the dough balls as needed.

5 Fill a large pot with about 2 inches (5 cm) of safflower or canola oil for frying and heat it over medium heat to about 325°F (170°C). Lower the heat to medium-low.

6 Use a slotted spoon to slip one Pon de Ring (parchment paper attached and down first) into the hot oil. Fry for about 1 minute on one side, until golden brown. Flip over and carefully remove the used parchment paper with tongs and discard. Fry for another minute, until golden brown. Remove the donuts from the oil and drain them on absorbent paper. Repeat with the remaining Pon de Rings.

7 *Make the strawberry glaze.* In a bowl, add 1 cup (120 g) of confectioners' sugar. Mix in the melted butter and puréed strawberries until thoroughly combined. If the glaze is too runny, mix in more confectioners' sugar, up to 1 additional cup (120 g).

8 While the rings are still hot, dip them in the glaze and enjoy!

PREP TIME	40 MINUTES
COOK TIME	16 TO 20 MINUTES
YIELD	ABOUT 8 DONUTS

To make matcha mochi beignets, substitute matcha for all the black sesame powder. Adjust to taste.

Black Sesame Mochi Beignets

Using black sesame and mochi, we'll transform classic beignets. I bet you'll be *mochi* in love when you bite into one of these to-die-for light and chewy beignets.

This recipe was adapted from one found on SAB by Ryan Lee (@butfirst.boba on Instagram). When Ryan presented his beautiful matcha mochi beignets, I just had to re-create them. Thank you very *matcha* for the inspiration, Ryan!

FOR THE BEIGNETS

¾ cup plus 1½ table-spoons (200 g) milk or soy milk

1 teaspoon instant yeast

¼ cup (60 g) silken tofu (or 1 egg [about 2 ounces, or 50 g])

1 tablespoon (14 g) butter, melted

3 tablespoons (39 g) granulated sugar

1 teaspoon miso

1 teaspoon vanilla extract (optional)

2 cups (250 g) all-purpose flour, sifted

½ cup (60 g) glutinous rice flour, sifted

2 tablespoons (16 g) tapioca flour, sifted

3 tablespoons (45 g) black sesame powder, adjust to taste

Neutral oil for frying, such as canola or safflower

FOR THE BLACK SESAME SUGAR

1 tablespoon (15 g) black sesame powder

¼ cup (30 g) confectioners' sugar

FOR THE DIPPING SAUCE

2 tablespoons (30 g) hot water

1 tablespoon (8 g) cornstarch, sifted

About ¾ cup (175 g) heavy cream

⅓ cup (67 g) granulated sugar

1 teaspoon vanilla extract (optional)

¼ teaspoon miso

1 tablespoon (15 g) black sesame powder

1 *Make the beignets.* In a stand mixer fitted with the paddle attachment, add all the beignet ingredients and mix on medium-low speed until a smooth dough forms, scraping down the bowl as needed. It's okay if the dough is sticky. Lightly flour your hands. Shape the dough into a ball. Transfer to a lightly greased bowl. Cover and let rise until the dough doubles in size, about 2 hours.

2 *Make the black sesame sugar.* Combine the black sesame powder and confectioners' sugar in a bowl and set aside.

3 *Make the dipping sauce.* Whisk together the hot water and cornstarch in a small saucepan. Mix in the rest of the dipping sauce ingredients, place over medium heat, and continuously whisk until the sauce thickens slightly, about 8 minutes. Remove from heat. Sieve the sauce through a fine mesh strainer as needed. Transfer the sauce to a serving bowl, cover, and cool completely in the refrigerator.

4 In a large pot, add 2½ inches (6.5 cm) of neutral oil. Heat over medium heat.

5 Transfer the dough to a floured work surface. With a floured rolling pin, flatten and roll out the dough into a large, ¼ inch (6 mm)-thick rectangle. Cut out 2-inch (5 cm) squares of dough.

6 Once the oil has reached about 370°F (188°C), fry the beignets, a few at a time, over medium-low heat. Cook one side for about 1 minute before flipping to the other side. When both sides are golden brown, remove the beignets from the oil with a slotted spoon and drain on absorbent paper.

7 Sprinkle the premixed sugar over the beignets. Ideally, serve them hot with the dipping sauce. Store any leftover beignets in an airtight container and consume within a few days. Reheat in the oven at 350°F (180°C, or gas mark 4) for 5 minutes.

PREP TIME	30 MINUTES
INACTIVE TIME	2 HOURS
COOK TIME	30 MINUTES
YIELD	25 TO 30 BEIGNETS

Soft Crumb Ube White Chocolate Scones

How gorgeous are these violet-colored scones? Feel free to generously drizzle heavenly hot honey over them. I hope *ube* (you'll be) impressed! (Have I always been this *punny?*)

This recipe is inspired by two recipes: one found on SAB by Karen Valles Sahagun of Karen's Take and one by Lisa Gnat of Bite Me More.

FOR THE SCONES

About 2⅔ cups (330 g)
all-purpose flour

⅓ cup (67 g)
granulated sugar

1 tablespoon (14 g)
baking powder

½ cup (1 stick, or 112 g)
super cold or frozen
butter, cubed

Optional mix-ins of
choice (such as 1 cup of
[160 g] white or [240 g]
dark chocolate, [145 g]
raisins, or [145 g] nuts)

1 egg (about 2 ounces,
or 50 g)

About ½ cup (75 g)
mashed cooked ube
(see the Greatest Ube
Halaya Jam recipe
on page 28)

½ cup (120 g)
buttermilk or milk

1 teaspoon miso

1 teaspoon vanilla
extract

1 teaspoon ube extract

FOR THE EGG WASH

1 egg (about 2 ounces,
or 50 g), beaten

Turbinado or demerara
sugar for sprinkling
(optional)

FOR THE HOT HONEY SAUCE

About ¾ cup
plus 1 tablespoon
(255 g) honey

1 to 2 habanero peppers
(or any peppers with a
kick will do)

½ teaspoon
apple cider vinegar

1 Line a large baking sheet with parchment paper.

2 In a large mixing bowl, sift together the flour, sugar, and baking powder. Add the butter. Using a pastry cutter or a fork, chop the butter into the dry ingredients until you have pea-sized fragments that are well distributed. Alternatively, hand rub and pinch the butter into the flour. The butter fragments do not all have to be the same size, just no bigger than peas.

3 If adding any optional mix-ins, fold them in now.

4 In a separate mixing bowl, whisk together the egg, ube, buttermilk, miso, and extracts until fully combined. Incorporate the wet ingredients into the dry ingredients and mix until a dough forms.

5 Turn the dough out onto the prepared pan and lightly flour your hands. Gently knead the dough, just until all the flour is incorporated. Mold the dough into a 1 inch (2.5 cm)-thick disc. Cut into eight to twelve wedges (like a pie or pizza). Freeze for about 30 minutes uncovered.

6 Preheat the oven to 425°F (220°C, or gas mark 7) and place a rack in the center.

7 *Make the hot honey sauce.* Add the honey and pepper(s) to a small saucepan and heat over medium-low heat until the honey simmers. Remove from the heat and stir in the vinegar. Cool and transfer to a glass jar or airtight container.

8 Brush the scones with the egg wash. Sprinkle with sugar, if desired. Bake for 10 minutes before lowering the heat to 350°F (180°C, or gas mark 4) and bake for another 15 minutes, until the tops are golden brown.

9 Remove from the oven and cool completely. Drizzle with hot honey and enjoy!

Instead of peppers, use ½ to 1 teaspoon of gochujang paste to make the hot honey sauce.

PREP TIME	25 MINUTES, PLUS 30 MINUTES TO FREEZE THE SCONE DOUGH
COOK TIME	30 TO 35 MINUTES
YIELD	8 TO 12 SCONES

Try using my Super Easy Milk Bread dough (page 100) to make these buns.

Tangzhong Milk Bread Five-Spice Cinnamon Buns

Tangzhong is a roux made from cooking water (or milk) and flour. Like a sponge, tangzhong helps bread retain more water during and after baking, resulting in these irresistibly fluffy, pillowy, and flavorful buns that remain soft and tender for days.

This recipe is adapted from one found on SAB by Shirley Chu (@simplechuoice on Instagram).

FOR THE TANGZHONG

About ¼ cup (30 g) all-purpose flour

½ cup (120 g) milk

FOR THE DOUGH

1 packet (2¼ teaspoons, or 7 to 8 g) active dry yeast

About ½ cup (115 g) warm milk (about 110°F [43°C])

About 2⅓ cups (325 g) bread flour

¼ cup plus 2 tablespoons (76 g) granulated sugar

½ teaspoon salt

1 egg (about 2 ounces, or 50 g)

2 tablespoons (28 g) butter, melted

FOR THE OPTIONAL EGG WASH

1 egg (about 2 ounces, or 50 g), beaten

FOR THE FILLING

½ cup (115 g) packed brown sugar

1 tablespoon (7 g) cinnamon, adjust to taste

¼ teaspoon five-spice powder, adjust to taste

¼ cup (½ stick, or 55 g) butter, softened

1 teaspoon miso

FOR THE FROSTING

3 ounces (85 g) cream cheese, softened

¼ cup (½ stick, or 55 g) butter, softened

1 teaspoon vanilla extract

¼ teaspoon miso or salt

A pinch of nutmeg or allspice (optional)

1 cup plus 1 tablespoon (128 g) confectioners' sugar, adjust to taste

1 *Make the tangzhong.* In a saucepan over low heat, add the flour and milk and whisk until no lumps remain. Once thickened like smooth mashed potatoes, remove from heat, cover, and cool.

2 *Mix the dough.* Add the yeast and a dash of sugar to the warm milk. Let the mixture foam and bubble for a few minutes. In a stand mixer fitted with the dough hook attachment, add the milk mixture, tangzhong, bread flour, sugar, salt, egg, and melted butter. Mix on low speed for a few minutes, until a smooth and elastic dough forms.

3 Flour your hands and shape the dough into a ball. Transfer to a lightly greased bowl. Cover and proof for 60 minutes, until roughly doubled in size.

4 *Make the filling.* Combine all the filling ingredients and mix until incorporated. Set aside.

5 Line a 9 x 13-inch (23 x 33 cm) baking pan with parchment paper.

6 Deflate the dough. Transfer to a floured work surface. Use a floured rolling pin to roll the dough into a rectangle about 15 x 9 inches (38 x 23 cm), while maintaining an even thickness.

7 Spread the filling evenly over the entire dough.

8 Roll into a jelly roll. With the seam-side down, slice into nine even 1-inch (2.5 cm) portions with a sharp knife.

9 Place all the buns, cut-side up, on the prepared pan in a three-by-three array. Cover and let rise for about 60 minutes, until puffy.

10 About 30 minutes before baking, preheat the oven to 350°F (180°C, or gas mark 4) with a rack in the center.

11 Brush the optional egg wash evenly over the buns. Bake for 25 to 30 minutes, until golden brown. Cool for a few minutes on the pan and then cool completely on a wire rack.

12 *Make the frosting.* In a stand mixer fitted with the paddle attachment, beat all the frosting ingredients (except the sugar) on medium-high speed until light and fluffy. Sift in the sugar, in increments, and beat until smooth. Spread the frosting over the buns and enjoy!

For an added kick and texture, try topping the buns with minced candied ginger.

PREP TIME	15 MINUTES
INACTIVE TIME	2 HOURS
COOK TIME	30 MINUTES
YIELD	9 BUNS

Brazos de Mercedes Meringue Swirls

My mother-in-law, Lilanie Young, makes the best *Brazos de Mercedes,* an airy and sweet meringue roll hailing from the Philippines. I dedicate these Brazos de Mercedes meringue swirls to her.

Creamy condensed milk custard (purple thanks to ube extract) tops these billowy meringue swirls. The tang from the calamansi zest counterbalances the sweetness of the meringue and custard. If you don't have calamansi, simply use the zest from any lemon or lime.

Note: These meringues need to dry out in the oven for at least 8 hours.

FOR THE CUSTARD

1 tablespoon (15 g) milk

½ teaspoon cornstarch

2 egg yolks (about 1½ ounces, or 40 g)

¼ cup (76 g) sweetened condensed milk

¼ teaspoon miso

½ teaspoon calamansi (or lemon) zest

1 teaspoon ube extract

1 tablespoon (14 g) butter, softened

FOR THE STIFF PEAKS MERINGUE

4 egg whites (about 4 ounces, or 120 g), room temperature

¼ teaspoon cream of tartar

½ cup (100 g) granulated sugar

FOR THE MERINGUE FOLD-INS

1 teaspoon cornstarch, sifted

¼ cup (30 g) confectioners' sugar, sifted

½ teaspoon calamansi or lemon juice

1 Line a large baking sheet with parchment paper and spray with cooking spray.

2 Preheat the oven to 175°F (80°C, or gas mark ¼) and place a rack in the lower third of the oven.

3 *Make the custard.* In a bowl, mix the milk and cornstarch until combined. In a saucepan over low heat, whisk together the egg yolks, condensed milk, miso, calamansi zest, and ube extract. Stir continuously until the mixture thickens. Add the milk and cornstarch mixture and whisk until homogenous. Continue to cook and stir the mixture until the custard thickens and pulls away from the pan when stirred. Scrape the pan to incorporate thicker portions of the custard. Remove from heat, add the butter, and mix until homogeneous. Transfer to a bowl, cover, and refrigerate for 30 minutes.

4 *Make the stiff peaks meringue (see technique on page 18).* Add the meringue ingredients. Use a flexible spatula to gently fold in and combine.

5 Scoop out mounds of the meringue onto the prepared baking sheet, making eight equal rounds, about 3 inches (7.5 cm) in diameter each.

6 Add drops (or dots) of cooled custard on top of each meringue. Using chopsticks (or a butter knife), dip into the meringue and swirl the custard around, starting with a small *O* shape in the center and swirling outward. You want to end up with purple swirls covering the surface of the meringue, and this takes some practice and deft flicks of the wrist.

7 Bake for 4 hours. Turn off the oven. With the door ajar, dry out the meringues in the oven for at least 8 hours or overnight. If the meringue appears too soft or chewy, bake again for 30 minutes at 175°F (80°C, or gas mark ¼).

PREP TIME	**30 MINUTES**
INACTIVE TIME	**8 HOURS TO OVERNIGHT**
COOK TIME	**4 HOURS**
YIELD	**8 MERINGUES**

Airy and Not-Too-Sweet Cakes

Would you believe me if I told you I baked my first cake when I was four years old? My own birthday cake, in fact! It's entirely true if you consider cracking and dropping a few eggs baking. Okay, I'll stop stretching the truth here; it was *Ah Ma,* my paternal grandmother, who baked the cake. To this day, I still remember the taste and texture of that fresh cream and fruit chiffon cake. To me, Ah Ma's cake will always be the epitome of an ideal Asian cake: fluffy and light as air, fresh and creamy, and not too sweet. We'll be re-creating her cake on page 96, and hopefully, she'll be proud of it!

Before we move on to the recipes, I must mention my Cottony Japanese Cheesecake (page 82). Back in 2017, this was the cake that started my baking obsession. I've written an entire post on how to troubleshoot this cake on my blog (modernasianbaking.com). A perfect Japanese cheesecake is tantalizing. It's soft, subtly cheesy, jiggly, delicious, and simply heavenly. Like the Pandan Chiffon Cake (page 86) and Pillowy Taiwanese Castella Cake (page 92), my Japanese cheesecake is based on whipped eggs.

For whatever occasion, or when you're feeling nostalgic, you can't go wrong with the Asian and Asian-inspired cakes in this section. I'm betting there'll be at least one cake here you'll become obsessed with. May it nurture your love for baking.

Spicy Gochujang Flourless Chocolate Cake

All at once spicy, sweet, and savory, the beloved Korean condiment, *gochujang*, makes this dessert incredibly special. The kick of spice and added umami make my favorite chocolate cake even more irresistible. Each fudgy spoonful dissolves in the mouth like thick hot chocolate. Surprisingly easy to bake at home, this decadent gluten-free cake is terrific for my tastebuds (but terrible for my waistline).

Note: If gochujang is not readily available, replace it with ¼ teaspoon of chili powder or cayenne pepper.

If you're feeling adventurous, substitute the gochujang with sriracha and let me know what you think.

FOR THE CAKE

About ¾ cup (175 g) bittersweet or semisweet chocolate

½ cup (1 stick, or 112 g) butter, cut into small cubes

¼ cup (50 g) granulated sugar

About ¼ cup (59 g) hot water

1 teaspoon cornstarch

3 medium eggs (about 5 ounces, or 150 g), beaten

1 tablespoon (20 g) gochujang paste

1 teaspoon vanilla extract

FOR THE OPTIONAL TOPPINGS

1 tablespoon (8 g) confectioners' sugar

Paprika for dusting

3 sliced strawberries

1 Line a 6-inch (15 cm) cake pan with a parchment circle. Nestle a strip of parchment paper into the sides of the cake pan to form a collar.

2 Preheat the oven to 300°F (150°C, or gas mark 2) and place a rack in the center. To prepare the water bath, place a baking dish that's large enough to hold the prepared baking pan on the oven rack. Pull the rack out and fill the dish with about 1 inch (2.5 cm) of hot water.

3 Melt the chocolate and butter using a double boiler or a pot over low heat. Whisk until the mixture is homogeneous. Add the sugar and whisk until the sugar dissolves. Scrape the bottom and sides of the pot with a flexible spatula. Remove from heat and set aside.

4 In a small bowl, add the hot water and cornstarch. Mix until the cornstarch dissolves. Add the hot water mixture to the chocolate mixture and whisk until combined. Add the eggs, gochujang paste, and vanilla extract to the batter and whisk until homogenous. The batter should be viscous and slick like thick chocolate syrup.

5 Pour the chocolate batter into the prepared pan. Bake in the prepared water bath for about 50 minutes, until the cake is almost set. Like cheesecake, a wobbly middle is desirable; however, if the cake appears too wet, bake for an additional 5 to 10 minutes.

6 Remove from the oven. Be careful of the hot steam from the oven. Cool completely before refrigerating for at least 4 hours. Transfer the cake onto a cake platter or serving plate. Garnish with the optional toppings of choice.

PREP TIME	15 MINUTES
COOK TIME	60 MINUTES
YIELD	ONE 6-INCH (15 CM) CAKE

Replace the matcha
with an equal amount
of cocoa, black sesame
powder, or hojicha pow-
der to change the flavor.
There's enough batter
for an 8-inch (20.5 cm)
cake; however, it will be
a shorter cake.

Dreamy Matcha Basque Cheesecake

In 1990, a Spanish chef named Santiago Rivera invented the Basque Burnt Cheese-cake. His homely yet beautiful dessert has transgressed cultural boundaries. It's no wonder I found Basque cheesecakes in bakeries across Japan, competing for my attention alongside Japanese Cheese-cakes. Basque Cheesecakes demand very little from us bakers. We burn them at high temperatures and deny them of crusts. Still, they reward us with rich dark tops, tantalizing flavors, and dreamy-creamy centers. By adding matcha here, we get a rustic cake with a beautiful jade center and a subtle leafy flavor.

RECIPE SPECS

FOR THE CAKE

About 1½ cups (337 g) cream cheese, cubed

¼ cup (½ stick, or 55 g) cold butter, cut into small cubes

½ cup (100 g) granulated sugar

3 medium eggs (about 5 ounces, or 150 g)

1 teaspoon miso

2 tablespoons (16 g) cornstarch, sifted

About 2½ tablespoons (20 g) cake flour (leave out for a gluten-free cheesecake), sifted

1 to 2 tablespoons (6 to 12 g) matcha

½ cup (120 g) milk

½ cup (120 g) heavy cream

1 teaspoon vanilla extract (optional)

FOR THE TOPPINGS

1 teaspoon confectioners' sugar for dusting

3 strawberries, sliced or other fruit of choice (optional)

1 Preheat the oven to 450°F (230°C, or gas mark 8) and place a rack in the center. Crumple a large sheet of parchment paper into a ball and unfurl it. Line the interior of a 6-inch (15 cm) springform or baking pan with the parchment paper. At least 1 to 2 inches (2.5 to 5 cm) of the parchment paper should over-hang the pan's rim on all sides. If the parchment paper is not large enough, use two overlapping sheets.

2 Blend all the cake ingredients in a mixer or blender on low to medium speed for about 1 minute or until you get a smooth, homogenous batter. Rest the batter for 30 minutes in the refrigerator to get rid of air bubbles.

3 Alternatively, use a double boiler or microwave to soften the cream cheese and butter. Mix until smooth and creamy. Mix in the sugar until incorporated. Add the rest of the ingredients (except for the toppings) and combine.

4 Pour the batter into the prepared pan. Tap the cake pan against the kitchen counter. Use a whisk to gently smooth out the top of the cake batter. Bake for 20 to 25 minutes, until the top is dark brown but not black and the center still jiggles and wobbles but is not runny.

5 Remove the cake from the oven. The cake will immediately deflate. Allow it to cool completely at room temperature before refrigerating it for at least 4 hours. Alternatively, clear some room in your freezer. After allowing the cake to cool for about 5 minutes, freeze the cake for at least 3 hours.

6 If using a springform pan, release the springform when ready to serve. Remove the parchment paper. Dust the cake with confectioners' sugar and garnish with strawberries or other fruits of choice, if desired.

If the top cracks, once the cheesecake sets, the cracks will not be very noticeable. You can cover any imperfections with a dusting of matcha or confectioners' sugar.

PREP TIME	10 MINUTES
COOK TIME	35 MINUTES
YIELD	ONE 6-INCH (15 CM) CAKE

For a matcha version of this cake, substitute 1 to 2 tablespoons (8 to 16 g) of flour with matcha. Visit modernasianbaking.com for tips on how to make different versions of this cake and trouble-shooting tips.

Cottony Japanese Cheesecake

This recipe took me three years to perfect, so don't feel too discouraged if your Japanese cheesecake is not perfect the first time around. When a nearly perfect Japanese cheesecake comes out of the oven, it's an ethereal experience. You'll want to bake this airy, melt-in-your-mouth showstopper over and over again.

Note: Once refrigerated and "aged," the cake will transform into a denser yet still light cheesecake.

Depending if your oven runs too hot or too cold, you may need to adjust baking temperatures accordingly. If the top of the cake cracks, your oven may be running too hot. Try beating the meringue to firm peaks instead of stiff peaks.

FOR THE BATTER

About 1 cup (225 g) cream cheese

¼ cup (½ stick, or 55 g) butter

¼ cup (50 g) granulated sugar

5 eggs yolks (about 3½ ounces, or 100 g)

About ¼ cup (30 g) cake flour

2 tablespoons (16 g) cornstarch

½ teaspoon baking powder

1 teaspoon vanilla extract

1 teaspoon lemon juice

½ cup (120 g) milk

FOR THE STIFF PEAKS MERINGUE

5 egg whites (about 5½ ounces, or 150 g), room temperature

½ teaspoon cream of tartar

¼ cup (50 g) granulated sugar

FOR THE OPTIONAL TOPPING

1 tablespoon (8 g) confectioners' sugar

PREP TIME	30 MINUTES
COOK TIME	65 TO 75 MINUTES
YIELD	ONE 8-INCH (20.5 CM) CAKE

1 Line an 8-inch (20.5 cm) cake pan with a parchment paper circle. Nestle a strip of parchment paper into the sides of the cake pan to form a collar.

2 Preheat the oven to 320°F (160°C, or gas mark 3) and place a rack in the center.

3 *Make the batter.* In a pot over low heat, mix the cream cheese and butter until smooth and creamy. Remove from heat. Whisk in the sugar and egg yolks until incorporated. Add the flour, cornstarch, baking powder, vanilla extract, lemon juice, and milk and whisk until incorporated, scraping down the sides of the pot as needed. Set aside.

4 *Make the stiff peaks meringue (see technique on page 18).*

5 Add one-fifth of the meringue to the batter. Gently whisk until incorporated. Repeat two more times. Then pour all the batter into the bowl with the meringue. Using a whisk, gently fold the remaining meringue into the batter, until homogenous, thick, and creamy. There should be no white streaks remaining in the batter.

6 Pour the batter into the prepared pan. Tap the pan against the counter a few times. Swirl the whisk over the top of the cake to smooth it out. Put the pan in a large baking dish. Place the baking dish on the oven rack. With oven mitts on, pull the rack out. Fill the baking dish with about 1½ inches (3.8 cm) of hot water. Bake for about 18 minutes, until the cake rises a bit. Crack the oven door open slightly for 10 seconds. Lower the oven temperature to 285°F (140°C, or gas mark 1) and bake for an additional 50 to 60 minutes, until the top is golden brown.

7 With the door ajar, keep the cake in the oven for 20 minutes after baking.

8 Remove from the oven. The cake will deflate a little.

9 To remove the cake from the pan, place a plate over the cake. If the pan is still hot, use oven mitts. Flip the cake out onto the plate. While the cake is upside down, remove the parchment paper. Quickly place a serving plate on top of the cake (it's the bottom part of the cake). Carefully flip again. Alternatively, if the parchment collar is supportive enough, hold two opposite sides of the parchment collar and simply lift the cake out of the pan.

10 Dust with the optional confectioners' sugar. Serve while the cake is still warm and jiggly.

To make graham cracker crumbs, place graham crackers in a sandwich bag, seal it, and use a rolling pin to smash and roll over the crackers until they become crumbs. Alternatively, use a food processor.

Tri-Color Japanese-Style Matcha Cheesecake

This beautiful Japanese-style "rare" matcha cheesecake has an unforgettably smooth and creamy texture. Take it to any dinner party and it'll probably steal the show. An easy-to-make recipe, it requires no eggs or baking other than par-baking the crust in the beginning.

This recipe is inspired by one found on SAB by Megan Wai (@wairecipes on Instagram) who adapted a recipe found on tsujiriquebec.ca/en.

RECIPE SPECS

FOR THE CRUST

1 cup (84 g) graham cracker crumbs

3 tablespoons (45 g) butter, melted

Pinch of salt

FOR THE CHEESECAKE BATTER

3 tablespoons (45 g) water

2 teaspoons gelatin

1¼ cups (290 g) cream cheese, softened

½ cup (100 g) granulated sugar

1 teaspoon vanilla extract

½ cup plus 2 tablespoons (50 g) heavy cream

FOR THE MATCHA CHEESE LAYER

¼ cup (60 g) milk

2 teaspoons matcha

FOR THE MATCHA JELLY LAYER

½ teaspoon matcha, sifted

1 teaspoon gelatin

2 teaspoons granulated sugar

½ cup (120 g) water

FOR THE OPTIONAL TOPPINGS

Fruits of choice

Edible gold flakes

1 Preheat the oven to 350°F (180°C, or gas mark 4) and place a rack in the center.

2 *Make the crust.* In a bowl, mix all the crust ingredients together, until the mixture resembles wet sand. Transfer to a greased 6-inch (15 cm) springform pan. Using the back of a spoon or clean fingers, tightly press the mixture evenly over the bottom of the pan, covering all edges. Bake for about 10 minutes and then cool completely.

3 *Make the cheesecake batter.* Add the water and gelatin to a small microwave-safe bowl and heat in the microwave for 15 seconds. Mix to dissolve the gelatin.

4 In a blender, add the gelatin mixture and all the cheesecake batter ingredients. Blend on low speed until smooth and homogeneous. Divide the batter, pouring even portions into two separate bowls. Cover one bowl and set aside.

5 *Make the matcha layer.* In the second bowl, mix in the milk and matcha until incorporated and smooth. Pour into the prepared pan, cover, and freeze for 30 minutes.

6 Take the pan out of the freezer. Pour in the remaining cheesecake batter, cover, and refrigerate for 30 minutes.

7 About 10 minutes before you're ready to remove the cheesecake from the refrigerator, *make the matcha jelly layer.* Combine all the ingredients in a microwave-safe bowl and microwave for 10 seconds. Mix to dissolve all the gelatin in the water.

8 Remove the pan from the refrigerator and pour the matcha jelly mixture over the top of the cheesecake. Refrigerate for 4 hours, until the cheesecake sets.

9 Release the springform and remove the cheesecake. Garnish with fruits of your choice, such as sliced strawberries. Decorate with optional sprinkling of edible gold flakes.

PREP TIME	15 MINUTES
COOK TIME	8 TO 10 MINUTES
YIELD	ONE 6-INCH (15 CM) CAKE

For the Asian Bakery Fresh Cream Cake recipe (page 96), substitute the pandan extract with vanilla extract.

Pandan Chiffon Cake

From the late 1930s to early 1940s, Ah Ma learned culinary secrets from restaurants in Vietnam. She passed down only one written recipe, a lemon chiffon cake recipe that I always turn to and treasure. I use about half of the ingredients she used in her recipe, and instead of lemon, this regal cloud of a cake is pandan-flavored.

FOR THE YOLK BATTER

About ⅓ cup (75 g) canola or vegetable oil

About ¾ cup (100 g) cake flour, sifted

About ⅓ cup (75 g) coconut milk (or any milk)

6 egg yolks (about 4 ounces, or 120 g)

1 teaspoon baking powder

1 teaspoon green pandan extract

2 tablespoons (26 g) granulated sugar

FOR THE FIRM PEAKS MERINGUE

6 egg whites (about 6½ ounces, or 180 g), room temperature

2 teaspoons lemon juice

⅔ cup (80 g) confectioners' sugar

1 Preheat the oven to 325°F (170°C, or gas mark 3) and place a rack in the center.

2 *Make the yolk batter.* Heat the oil in a saucepan over medium heat, until it reaches about 176°F (80°C). Remove from heat. Add the cake flour and whisk until combined. Transfer the mixture to a large bowl, cover, and cool for a few minutes. Mix in the coconut milk. Add the egg yolks, baking powder, pandan extract, and sugar and whisk until combined and smooth. Set aside.

3 *Make the firm peaks meringue (see technique on page 18).*

4 *Make the final batter.* Add one-fourth of the meringue to the yolk batter. Gently whisk until incorporated. Add another fourth of the meringue to the yolk batter and whisk until incorporated. Then pour all the batter into the bowl with the remaining meringue. Use a flexible spatula to gently fold the meringue into the batter, until homogenous, thick, and creamy. There should be no white streaks remaining in the batter. If stubborn lumps of meringue remain, use a whisk to gently mix them into the final batter.

5 Pour the batter into an ungreased 9-inch (23 cm) tube pan. Tap the pan against the counter a few times. Smooth out the top of the batter with the whisk.

6 Spray a large sheet of aluminum foil with cooking spray and place it over the top of the pan. Bake the cake for 25 minutes. Carefully remove the aluminum foil. Reduce the temperature to 310°F (155°C, or gas mark 2). Bake for an additional 20 to 25 minutes, until thoroughly cooked and golden brown. Insert a bamboo stick into the cake. If it comes out clean, the cake is ready.

7 Remove the cake from the oven. From a height of about 3 inches (7.5 cm) above the counter, drop the cake pan down to shock the cake. Repeat two more times.

8 Invert the pan and place the tube on a lidded jar or an inverted cup. Cool completely before removing the cake from the pan. Be patient as this can take a few hours. Run a knife gently along the edges where the cake adheres to the tube pan to remove the cake.

Enjoy a slice with hot tea. While this cake is lovely on its own, feel free to serve it with a jam of your choice, honey, or whipped cream.

PREP TIME	20 MINUTES
COOK TIME	50 TO 55 MINUTES
YIELD	ONE 9-INCH (23 CM) CAKE

Try omitting the instant coffee and spread honey or jam over your cake instead of cream. Or substitute the instant coffee with 1 tablespoon (6 g) of matcha to make a matcha swiss roll cake.

Chinese Bakery Swiss Roll Cake

Swiss roll cakes from Chinese bakeries are soft and light as air, not too sweet, and perfect for my taste buds. I love coffee-flavored cakes, so we'll be making a coffee sponge cake.

RECIPE SPECS

FOR THE BATTER

4 egg yolks (about 3 ounces, or 80 g)

2 tablespoons plus 1 teaspoon (30 g) granulated sugar

1 teaspoon vanilla extract

¼ teaspoon salt

1 tablespoon (3 g) instant coffee

1½ tablespoons hot water (25 g)

3 tablespoons (45 g) vegetable or canola oil

About ½ cup (60 g) cake flour

½ teaspoon baking powder

FOR THE SOFT PEAKS MERINGUE

4 egg whites (about 4 ounces, or 120 g), room temperature

¼ teaspoon vinegar (optional)

3 tablespoons (39 g) granulated sugar

FOR THE CREAM FILLING

½ cup (120 g) heavy cream

2 tablespoons (26 g) granulated sugar

1 teaspoon vanilla extract

PREP TIME	**20 MINUTES**
COOK TIME	**ABOUT 20 TO 25 MINUTES**
YIELD	**ONE 9 INCH (23 CM)-LONG CAKE**

1 Line a 9 x 13-inch (23 x 33 cm) baking pan with parchment paper.

2 Preheat the oven to 350°F (180°C, or gas mark 4) and place a rack in the center.

3 *Make the batter.* In a large bowl, whisk the egg yolks, sugar, vanilla extract, and salt until incorporated. Dissolve the instant coffee in the hot water and mix it into the batter. In a small bowl, combine the oil and flour until incorporated. Add the oil and flour mixture to the batter, along with the baking powder, and mix until fully combined. Set aside.

4 *Make the soft peaks meringue (see technique on page 18).*

5 Using a whisk, gently mix one-third of the meringue in the batter, until incorporated. Repeat with another third of the meringue. Using a flexible spatula, gently fold the final portion of the meringue into the batter until fully incorporated. The resulting batter should be creamy and homogeneous, like a thick and smooth coffee milkshake, with no white streaks of meringue remaining. Pour the batter into the prepared pan. Tap the pan against the counter a few times. Smooth and even out the cake with a pastry scraper. Bake for about 20 to 25 minutes, until the cake rises and the top is golden. You don't want to overbake this sponge cake.

6 Clean and dry a stand mixer bowl and whisk attachment. Remove the cake from the oven. Flip it out onto the lined baking sheet. Peel off the parchment paper used in the oven.

7 Using the new parchment paper, immediately roll the shorter end of the cake into a 9 inch (23 cm)-long jelly roll. During this first roll, you want the cake to be hot to warm. Cover and set aside to cool.

8 *Make the cream filling.* In a stand mixer fitted with a whisk attachment, whip all the filling ingredients on medium-high speed until stiff peaks form, about 5 minutes.

9 Unroll the cake. Spread the cream evenly over it, tapering at the ends with less cream and leaving a ½-inch (1.3 cm) border on all sides. Re-roll into a jelly roll (without the parchment paper), encasing the cream in the center. Remove any extra cream that piles up toward the end. With the seam-side down, wrap the cake in parchment paper and tie or tape the ends of the parchment paper.

10 Refrigerate for at least 4 hours. Slice off the ends of the cake. Cut into 1 inch (2.5 cm)-thick slices and serve.

For added flair, top the cake with cooked boba (page 32).

Crème Brûlée Mille-Crêpes Cake

Although crêpes originated in France, it was a Japanese pâtissier named Emy Wada who invented mille-crêpes cakes in the eighties. Mille-crêpes cakes are known for impressive layers of feathery-light crêpes smothered in rich cream. Here's a crème brûlée mille-crêpes cake with a glassy burnt top and layers of luscious diplomat cream, making it a truly subtly Asian cake.

This stunner of a cake is a labor of love that'll demand a lot of your patience and time. Like all great things, however, it'll be worth it!

This recipe is inspired by one found on SAB by Mai Nguyen (@mai.ng on Instagram).

RECIPE SPECS

FOR THE CRÊPES BATTER

4 medium eggs (about 7 ounces, or 200 g), room temperature

½ cup (120 g) hot water

1 cup (235 g) milk

¼ cup (60 g) melted and browned butter

¼ teaspoon miso or a pinch of salt

1 teaspoon vanilla extract

2 tablespoons (26 g) granulated sugar

About 1¼ cups (150 g) all-purpose flour, sifted

FOR THE DIPLOMAT CREAM FILLING

1 recipe *crème pâtissière* (see page 123), omit the spices

½ cup (120 g) heavy cream

2 tablespoons (16 g) confectioners' sugar

FOR THE CRÈME BRÛLÉE TOP

Granulated sugar

1 *Make the crêpes batter.* Starting with the wet ingredients, add all the crêpes batter ingredients to a blender and mix on medium speed until fully incorporated and smooth. Use a flexible spatula to scrape down the sides of the blender bowl as needed. Sieve the batter through a fine-mesh strainer into a large bowl. Cover and refrigerate for at least 4 hours or overnight.

2 *Make the diplomat cream filling.* Make the crème pâtissière and refrigerate for at least 1 hour. In a stand mixer fitted with the paddle attachment, whip the heavy cream and confectioners' sugar to medium peaks.

3 Stir the cold crème pâtissière with a flexible spatula until smooth. Gently fold the whipped cream into the crème pâtissière in three additions. Set aside or refrigerate until you are ready to assemble the crêpes cake.

4 *Make the mille-crêpes cake.* Heat a lightly buttered 9-inch (23 cm) skillet over medium heat. Add 3 to 4 tablespoons (45 to 60 g) of batter. Tip the pan to evenly coat the entire bottom surface. Cook both sides until golden brown, about 30 seconds on the first side and 15 seconds on the second side. Rest the crêpe on parchment paper or a wire rack. Repeat until you've used up the batter, making fifteen to sixteen crêpes. Cool the crêpes completely.

5 *Assemble the mille-crêpes cake.* Transfer one crêpe to a serving plate. Spread a thin layer of diplomat cream over the crêpe. Continue adding crêpe and cream layers. End with a crêpe layer.

6 Cover the cake with plastic wrap and refrigerate for 2 to 4 hours.

7 Remove the cake from the refrigerator. Dust the top evenly with sugar. Use a kitchen blowtorch to caramelize the top.

8 Store any leftover cake in the refrigerator and consume within a few days. You can freeze this cake for up to 3 months.

PREP TIME	**OVER AN HOUR**
INACTIVE TIME	**UP TO OVERNIGHT**
COOK TIME	**OVER AN HOUR**
YIELD	**ONE 9-INCH (23 CM) CAKE**

For a less eggy taste, add a teaspoon of lemon or yuzu juice to the batter.

Pillowy Taiwanese Castella Cake

This Taiwanese castella cake is a super-aerated sponge cake, relying solely on whipping meringue to soft peaks for leavening. As it melts in your mouth, you may wonder, is it really a cake or baked foam?

The *Pão de Castela* (bread of Castile), first baked during the sixteenth century in Portugal, inspired the creation of Asian-style castella cakes.

RECIPE SPECS

FOR THE YOLK BATTER

¼ cup (½ stick) plus 1 tablespoon (70 g) unsalted butter

⅓ cup (80 g) milk

About ½ cup (70 g) cake flour, sifted

¼ teaspoon miso or salt

5 egg yolks (about 3½ ounces, or 100 g), beaten

¼ cup (50 g) granulated sugar

1 teaspoon vanilla extract

FOR THE SOFT PEAKS MERINGUE

5 egg whites (about 5½ ounces, or 150 g), room temperature

½ teaspoon cream of tartar

¼ cup (50 g) granulated sugar

FOR THE OPTIONAL TOPPINGS

Confectioners' sugar for dusting

Honey for drizzling

Sliced fruits of choice

1 Line the entire interior of a square 6-inch (15 cm) cake pan with a large piece of parchment paper, folded at the corners. (Ideally, the cake pan is 3 inches, or 7.5 cm, tall.)

2 Preheat the oven to 320°F (160°C, or gas mark 3) and place a rack in the center.

3 *Make the yolk batter.* In a saucepan over medium heat, heat the butter until it melts and starts to bubble. Add the milk and mix to combine. Remove from heat. Add the cake flour and miso (or salt) and whisk until a smooth batter forms. Pour the mixture into a large bowl. Add the egg yolks, sugar, and vanilla extract and whisk until fully incorporated and smooth. Set aside.

4 *Make the soft peaks meringue (see technique on page 18).*

5 *Make the final batter.* Add one-fourth of the meringue to the yolk batter. Gently whisk until incorporated. Repeat one more time and then pour all the batter into a bowl. Using a flexible spatula, gently fold the remaining meringue into the batter, until homogenous and creamy and no white streaks or meringue lumps remain. Using a whisk to gently mix the batter is okay at this point.

6 Pour the batter into the prepared pan. Put the pan in a large baking dish. Place the baking dish on the oven rack. With oven mitts on, pull the rack out. Fill the baking dish with about 1 inch (2.5 cm) of hot water. Bake for about 60 to 65 minutes, until the cake rises and the top is golden brown. Keep the cake in the oven, with the door ajar, for about 10 minutes after baking.

7 Remove the cake from the oven. The cake should deflate just a little, and the top may become a bit wrinkly.

8 The easiest way to remove the cake is to hold two sides of the parchment paper and pull the cake out of the pan with the parchment paper supporting it. Be sure to remove the wet parchment paper.

9 Garnish the cake with the optional ingredients.

Some bakers swear by dropping the cake pan down from a height of about 3 inches (7.5 cm) immediately after removing the cake from the oven. I feel this cake may be too fragile for drop shocking.

PREP TIME	20 MINUTES
COOK TIME	60 MINUTES
YIELD	ONE 6-INCH (15 CM) CAKE

SAB Member Joedy Tran (@nuocmamafoods on Instagram) recommends using a blender to mix the batter. After all the sugar dissolves in the saucepan, transfer the mixture to a blender. Add the eggs and baking powder last and blend until just combined. This way, you can skip using the strainer. Thank you, Joedy, for helping me perfect this recipe!

One-Pot Honeycomb Cake

nướng   ưu ớon

Honeycomb cake, known as *bánh bò nướng* in Vietnam and *bika ambon* in Indonesia, is a beloved Southeast Asian dessert. On the outside, this cake looks like any other Bundt cake with its golden-brown crust. Once sliced, you'll see a vibrant shade of green and beautiful honeycomb pattern.

Note: Making this cake, you'll have to move and work quickly. Please read through the recipe first.

RECIPE SPECS

FOR THE CAKE

1¾ cups plus 2 tablespoons (240 g) tapioca flour, sifted

3 tablespoons (30 g) rice flour, sifted

1 14-oz (400 g) can coconut milk

1 cup (200 g) granulated sugar

¼ cup (60 g) coconut water or water

1 tablespoon (16 g) miso

1 teaspoon green pandan extract

1 teaspoon vanilla extract (optional)

2 tablespoons (28 g) butter, melted

7 medium eggs (about 12 ounces, or 350 g), room temperature

2 tablespoons plus 1 teaspoon (32 g) baking powder, sifted

¼ teaspoon cream of tartar

FOR THE OPTIONAL TOPPINGS

Confectioners' sugar

Coconut flakes

1 Preheat the oven to 350°F (180°C, or gas mark 4) with a rack in the center. Place a 9-inch (23 cm) Bundt or cake pan in the oven.

2 In a heavy saucepan, add the tapioca flour, rice flour, coconut milk, sugar, coconut water or water, miso, pandan extract, optional vanilla extract, and melted butter and whisk to combine. While continuously whisking, heat over medium heat until all the sugar dissolves and the mixture is homogeneous. Rest for 5 minutes.

3 Then crack the eggs directly into the saucepan. Cut each yolk in halves or quarters using clean scissors. Whisk the mixture gently until all the eggs are barely incorporated. Add the baking powder and cream of tartar and whisk until just combined. Some lumps are okay.

4 You'll need to work quickly now. Using oven mitts, remove the preheated pan from the oven. Generously grease the entire interior of the pan with cooking spray or neutral oil. With a fine-mesh strainer, carefully sieve all the batter directly into the pan. Use a spatula to press and direct the batter through the strainer as needed. The pan is still hot, so while still using an oven mitt, swirl the batter in the pan so it's evenly distributed in the pan.

5 Bake for 50 to 55 minutes, until the top is golden brown. Let the cake rest in the oven for 5 minutes. Then with the oven door slightly ajar, keep the cake in the oven for an additional 15 minutes. The cake will deflate a little.

6 Cool completely at room temperature. Dust with the optional confectioners' sugar or coconut flakes or both. Slice and serve.

PREP TIME	10 MINUTES
COOK TIME	50 TO 55 MINUTES
YIELD	ONE 9-INCH (23 CM) CAKE

After the whipped cream forms soft peaks, add a few drops of food coloring of your choice to change the color of the cream.

Asian Bakery Fresh Cream Cake (Ah Ma's Cake)

I always reminisce about the birthday cake Ah Ma made for me when I was turning five: light, fresh, snow-like cream blanketed layers of soft chiffon cake and fresh fruits. It was a cake just like the ones you would find in an Asian bakery in almost any Chinatown—not too sweet, ever so light, and unforgettably dreamy. Ah Ma, I hope I made you proud by re-creating your cake.

RECIPE SPECS

FOR THE CHIFFON CAKE

1 recipe Pandan Chiffon Cake (see page 86)

1 teaspoon vanilla extract

1 teaspoon lemon juice (optional)

FOR THE SIMPLE SYRUP

¼ cup (60 g) water

¼ cup (50 g) granulated sugar

1 teaspoon vanilla extract

Pinch of salt

FOR THE WHIPPED CREAM

2 teaspoons gelatin powder

2½ tablespoons (38 g) water

3 cups (705 g) heavy cream, very cold

⅓ cup (40 g) confectioners' sugar, sifted

1 teaspoon vanilla extract

FOR THE TOPPINGS

About 2 cups (300 g) sliced fresh fruits of choice, such as strawberries, kiwis, and mangos

Berries of choice (optional)

1 *Make the chiffon cake following the instructions on page 87,* making sure to substitute the pandan extract with 1 teaspoon of vanilla extract. Optionally, add 1 teaspoon of lemon juice to the batter. Bake in a 9 inch (23 cm) tube pan. Invert and cool completely.

2 *Make the simple syrup.* Mix all the ingredients in a heavy saucepan and heat until all the sugar dissolves. Cool completely.

Use a cake leveler or serrated knife to level the cake. Carefully divide the cake into two even layers. Generously brush the tops of both cake layers with the cooled syrup.

3 *Make the whipped cream.* In a bowl, add the gelatin and water and allow the gelatin to bloom (absorb the water and solidify). Heat in the microwave for 15 seconds, until the mixture liquefies. Allow to cool but not solidify. In a stand mixer fitted with the whisk attachment, add the heavy cream, confectioners' sugar, and vanilla extract and beat until soft peaks form. Drizzle in the liquid gelatin and beat on medium speed until the whipped cream is stabilized and stiff peaks form. Do not overwhip.

4 *Assemble the cake.* Add one cake layer to a cake board. Transfer to a revolving cake stand if you have one. Top the cake with a generous layer of whipped cream. Evenly place sliced fruits over the entire cream layer, as desired.

5 Add the second cake layer. Frost the entire cake with a thin layer of whipped cream. This is the crumb coat.

6 Frost the entire cake again, this time with a thicker layer.

7 Use a pastry scraper to smooth out the top and the sides of the cake.

8 Fill a piping bag (fitted with a tip of your choice) with whipped cream. Pipe designs and borders of your choice on the cake. Decorate the cake with fruits and fruit slices. Have fun!

9 Cover and refrigerate the cake until ready to serve.

PREP TIME	ABOUT 1 HOUR
COOK TIME	65 MINUTES
YIELD	ONE 9-INCH (23 CM) CAKE

Bread and
Yeasted Bakes

"Bread is like the sun, it rises in the yeast . . ."

For the longest time, I was not a bread person. I never enjoyed dry bread and tend to use bread as a vessel for way too much butter. Plus, I *loaf* it when bread sticks to my palate.

My stance on bread changed when I discovered milk bread. Soft, springy, tender, pillowy, sweet, feathery—if I could only have one bread for the rest of my life, it would undoubtedly be milk bread. I had always thought baking homemade bread would be the final frontier for me, but I actually baked bread before I baked cookies from scratch.

Although I cover different methods (tangzhong and yudane) of making milk bread dough, I recommend starting with my Super Easy Milk Bread recipe (page 100). Using my recipe, you'll be able to mix a versatile dough that can be transformed into loaves, buns, or rolls.

Although I would have loved to dedicate this entire section to milk bread, I've included other exciting bread and yeasted bakes recipes, such as a delicious Butter Basil Sourdough Naan made with sourdough starter (page 108). With the No-Knead Miso Focaccia recipe (page 116), you'll make a stunning and umami-packed bread that demands little from you other than time to rest and rise.

So get *bready,* my friend. Stop *loafing* around, and *crust* me with these recipes. They will not be *crumby!* (Oh, how I love bread puns. They can never get *stale* or *mold!* Okay, I'll stop now before I'm *toast.*)

To make a vegan version of this bread, use plant-based milk like oat milk or coconut milk, vegan butter, and about ¼ cup (60 g) of silken or soft tofu instead of the egg.

Super Easy Milk Bread

The irresistibly soft, springy, and sweet milk bread is a staple in Asian bakeries. Its versatile dough has endless potential. Use it to make your cinnamon buns, donuts, garlic knots, dinner rolls, and more!

My recipe does not require the yudane (page 105) or tangzhong (page 73) methods to achieve a surprisingly feathery and tender milk bread. Do try the other methods in this book though!

Note: Though this bread will take an entire morning or afternoon to make, it'll be worth it! Double the ingredients to make two loaves at a time.

RECIPE SPECS

FOR THE MILK BREAD DOUGH

¾ cup (175 g) milk

1 packet (2¼ teaspoons, or 7 to 8 g) active dry yeast

Dash of sugar

About 2½ cups (350 g) bread flour, sifted

¼ cup plus 2 table-spoons (76 g) granulated sugar

1 egg (about 2 ounces, or 50 g)

½ teaspoon salt

2 tablespoons (28 g) butter, softened

FOR THE EGG WASH

1 egg (about 2 ounces, or 50 g), beaten

1 *Make the milk bread dough.* Microwave the milk in 20-second bursts, until it reaches about 110°F (43°C). Stir in the yeast and a dash of sugar. Set aside for a few minutes.

2 In a stand mixer fitted with the dough hook attachment, combine the yeast mixture and, except for the butter, the remaining dough ingredients. Mix on low speed for a few minutes, until the dough is cohesive, sticky, and elastic. Cover and rest for 20 minutes. Then mix for about 9 minutes on low speed, adding the butter in increments and scraping down the sides of the bowl as needed, until a smooth, elastic dough forms. If it's tacky, that's okay, as this is a wetter dough. If it's too wet, add a little flour. Although my dough always passes the windowpane test at this point, if yours does not pass the test, it's fine as long as it's elastic, like stretchy chewed gum (refer to page 19 for the technique and how to troubleshoot this dough). Shape into a ball and cover.

(Please stop here if you are using this dough for another recipe. Otherwise, continue.)

3 Let rise for 60 minutes, until roughly doubled in size.

4 Butter a 9 x 5-inch (23 x 13 cm) loaf pan.

5 Deflate the dough and divide into three equal pieces.

6 With a floured rolling pin, roll each piece of dough into a long oval, about 10 inches (25.5 cm) long. Refer to the *shaping the milk bread dough* technique on page 20. Place each rolled dough, seam-side down and side by side, in the prepared pan.

7 Cover and proof for 60 minutes, until roughly doubled in size.

8 About 30 minutes before baking, preheat the oven to 350°F (180°C, or gas mark 4) with a rack in the center.

9 Brush egg wash evenly over the tops of each bun. (Alternatively, you can skip the egg wash and dust the loaves with bread flour instead.)

10 Bake for 30 to 35 minutes, until the tops are golden brown. At around 15 minutes into baking, cover the bread with a sheet of aluminum foil so the bread doesn't get too dark.

11 Remove from the oven. I like to enjoy this bread immediately because that's when it is the softest and fluffiest.

PREP TIME	35 MINUTES
INACTIVE TIME	140 MINUTES
COOK TIME	30 TO 35 MINUTES
YIELD	1 LOAF OF BREAD

Reserve a small ball of dough to make little ears for the buns. Wet the ears and stick them on the bun dough. Use melted chocolate and a toothpick to draw cute faces.

Vegan Blueberry Milk Bread Pull-Apart Buns

When blueberries are in season, I love adding them to my cookie and bread dough. These soft, pillowy, plant-based buns are beautifully bluish-purple on the inside and packed with antioxidants and fiber.

RECIPE SPECS

FOR THE BUNS

About ½ cup (115 g) coconut milk

About ¾ cup (120 g) blueberries (blackberries work too)

1 packet (2¼ teaspoons, or 7 to 8 g) active dry yeast

Dash of sugar

About 2½ cups (350 g) bread flour, sifted

About 6 tablespoons (75 g) granulated sugar

1 teaspoon salt

1 teaspoon vanilla extract

1 tablespoon lemon zest

2 tablespoons (28 g) vegan butter, softened

FOR THE WASH

Plant-based milk or melted vegan butter

Bread flour for dusting

1 Add the coconut milk and blueberries to a blender and blend for a few seconds. You want some of the blueberry skin and flesh to remain intact, so don't blend into a smoothie or purée. Transfer the mixture to a microwave-safe bowl and heat in 20-second bursts to about 110°F (43°C). Mix in the yeast and a dash of sugar. Set aside for a few minutes, until the yeast bubbles and foams.

2 In a stand mixer fitted with the dough hook attachment, tip in the flour, sugar, and salt. Add the blueberry mixture, vanilla extract, and lemon zest. Mix on low speed until a tacky, elastic dough forms. Cover and rest for 20 minutes. Then mix for about 9 minutes on low speed, adding the butter in increments and scraping the bowl as needed, until a smooth, elastic dough forms. If it's tacky, that's okay, as this is a wetter dough. If it's too wet, add a little flour. You can perform the windowpane test with a small piece of dough. As long as the dough is stretchy and elastic, you can stop kneading. Shape into a ball and cover. Let rise until roughly doubled in size, about 60 minutes.

3 Grease (with vegan butter) or line an 8 x 8-inch (20.5 x 20.5 cm) baking pan with parchment paper.

4 Deflate the dough. Divide into nine equal pieces (about 75 g, or 2½ ounces, each). Working one at a time, make nine dough balls (refer to the *shaping milk bread buns* technique on page 21). Place the dough balls in the pan in a three-by-three array.

5 Proof until puffy and roughly doubled in size, about 60 minutes.

6 About 30 minutes before baking, preheat the oven to 350°F (180°C, or gas mark 4) and place a rack in the center.

7 Wash the tops with the vegan milk or melted butter and dust with bread flour. Bake for 30 to 35 minutes, until the edges of the buns are golden brown. At around 20 minutes into baking, cover with a sheet of aluminum foil.

8 Remove from the oven and cool on a wire rack.

Enjoy warm with a generous spreading of vegan butter or vegan maple butter.

PREP TIME	**35 MINUTES**
INACTIVE TIME	**120 MINUTES**
COOK TIME	**30 TO 35 MINUTES**
YIELD	**9 BUNS**

Although I prefer not to score the tops of these buns, you can score the cookie discs diagonally into crisscross patterns with a pastry scraper or cutter prior to baking.

Pineapple Buns

Pineapple buns (or *bolo bau*), a staple in Chinese bakeries, are named for the way they look. While you can fill them with pineapple jam, they're not made with any pineapple. I like these buns hot with a slab of butter wedged in the center.

This recipe is adapted from one found on SAB by Rebekah Wong (@wongs_pantry on Instagram).

Note: Here we'll use the yudane method (1:1 ratio of boiling water to flour) to make the milk bread buns.

FOR THE YUDANE

About ⅔ cup (80 g) all-purpose flour

⅓ cup (80 g) boiling water

Pinch of salt

FOR THE COOKIE CRUST DOUGH

¼ cup (½ stick, or 55 g) butter, room temperature

½ cup (100 g) granulated sugar

1 egg yolk (about ¾ ounce, or 20 g)

1 teaspoon miso

About 1 cup (120 g) all-purpose flour, sifted

½ teaspoon baking powder

½ teaspoon baking soda

FOR THE MILK BREAD DOUGH

About ½ cup plus 1 teaspoon (125 g) warm (110°F or 43°C) milk

¼ cup plus 2 tablespoons (75 g) granulated sugar

1 packet (2¼ teaspoons, or 7 to 8 g) active dry yeast

About 2¾ cups (350 g) all-purpose flour

1 egg (about 2 ounces, or 50 g), room temperature

½ teaspoon salt

2 tablespoons (28 g) butter, room temperature

FOR THE EGG WASH

2 egg yolks (about 1½ ounces, or 40 g), beaten

PREP TIME	30 MINUTES
INACTIVE TIME	140 MINUTES
COOK TIME	18 TO 20 MINUTES
YIELD	6 BUNS

1 *Make the yudane.* Combine the yudane ingredients in a bowl, cover, and refrigerate overnight.

2 *Make the cookie crust dough.* In a stand mixer fitted with the paddle attachment, beat the butter and sugar on medium-high until light and fluffy, about 2 minutes. Add the egg yolk and miso and mix until combined. Sift in the dry ingredients and mix until incorporated. If the dough is not coming together or if it is too dry, try adding a little milk, a teaspoon at a time, until a smooth, cohesive dough forms. Shape the dough into a log and cover in plastic wrap. Refrigerate for at least 60 minutes.

3 Line a large baking sheet with parchment paper.

4 *Make the milk bread dough.* Add the warm milk, a pinch of sugar, and the yeast to a bowl. Mix and set aside for a few minutes, until foamy. Except for the butter, add the remaining milk bread dough ingredients, the yudane, and the yeast mixture to a stand mixer fitted with the dough hook attachment. Mix on low speed until an elastic dough forms. Cover the dough and let rest for 20 minutes. Add the butter in increments and mix on low speed for a few minutes. Don't overmix.

5 Transfer the dough to a floured work surface and flour your hands. Knead the dough until it is smooth, elastic, and passes the windowpane test (refer to page 19 for the technique and how to troubleshoot bread dough). Cover and let rise until roughly doubled in size, about 60 minutes.

6 About 30 minutes before baking, preheat the oven to 350°F (180°C, or gas mark 4) and place a rack in the center.

7 Remove the cookie crust dough from the refrigerator. Let soften at room temperature for a few minutes. Transfer to a lightly floured work surface. Divide into six even portions. Shape each portion into a dough ball. Flatten each dough ball into a disc, about 2½ inches (6.5 cm) in diameter. These will be used later to drape the buns.

8 Deflate the milk bread dough. Transfer to a floured work surface and divide into six equal portions. Flour your hands and shape each piece into a smooth ball (see page 21).

9 Drape each bun with a cookie disc, pressing in the edges so the disc and the bun stick together.

10 Brush the egg wash evenly and generously over the tops of the buns. Give each bun space on the prepared baking sheet.

11 Bake for 18 to 20 minutes, until the tops are beautifully golden.

Try adding
½ teaspoon of
coconut extract
when making
the cream.

Coconut Cream Buns

Coconut cream buns are called *nai you bao* in Cantonese, which literally means "milk oil bun." Don't let this name fool you. Coconut cream buns are not oily, but tremendously satisfying and crave-worthy. They're a staple in Chinese bakeries and have always been my favorite Asian-style bun. Maybe it's because they were also my dad's favorite. A lifelong stoic, his face always lit up when he bit into a nai you bao.

RECIPE SPECS

FOR THE BREAD

1 recipe Super Easy Milk Bread dough (see page 100) or Tangzhong Milk Bread dough (see page 73)

1 egg (about 2 ounces, or 50 g), beaten, for egg wash

FOR THE GLAZE

2 tablespoons (26 g) granulated sugar

2 tablespoons (30 g) hot water

½ teaspoon vanilla extract

FOR THE CREAM

1 cup (235 g) heavy cream

½ teaspoon miso

3 tablespoons (24 g) confectioners' sugar

¼ teaspoon vanilla extract

3 tablespoons (45 g) butter, melted and cooled

FOR THE TOPPINGS

Coconut flakes or shredded coconut

Sea salt flakes for sprinkling (optional)

1 Line a large baking sheet with parchment paper.

2 *Make the milk bread dough,* cover, and let rise for 60 minutes, until roughly doubled in size. Deflate and transfer to a floured work surface. Divide the dough into eight even pieces. Shape each piece into an oval (or small football). Please refer to the technique on page 21.

3 Transfer the buns to the prepared baking sheet, giving each bun ample space. Use two lined baking sheets if needed. Proof for 60 minutes, until roughly doubled in size.

4 About 30 minutes before baking, preheat the oven to 350°F (180°C, or gas mark 4) and place a rack in the center.

5 Generously brush the buns with the egg wash. Bake the buns for 15 to 20 minutes, until the tops are golden brown.

6 *Make the glaze.* In a small bowl, mix the sugar, hot water, and vanilla extract together until the sugar dissolves.

7 *Make the cream.* In a stand mixer fitted with the whisk attachment, beat the heavy cream, miso, sugar, and vanilla extract until soft peaks form. Gradually add the melted butter, 1 tablespoon (15 g) at a time, and beat until stiff peaks form. Don't overmix. Transfer to a piping bag fitted with a star tip (or any tip) and refrigerate.

8 Remove the buns from the oven. While the buns are still hot, brush the glaze over the tops of the buns. Place the coconut flakes or shredded coconut in a shallow bowl. Carefully dip in the buns to coat with coconut. Let the buns cool. Slice each bun three-quarters of the way down the middle, lengthwise. Pipe the cream into each bun slit and on top of the slit. Sprinkle a bit of the optional sea salt flakes on top of the cream. Sprinkle on a bit more coconut.

Enjoy with a cup of tea.

PREP TIME	**25 MINUTES**
INACTIVE TIME	**120 MINUTES**
COOK TIME	**15 TO 20 MINUTES**
YIELD	**8 BUNS**

Butter Basil Sourdough Naan

Naan is a traditional Indian leavened flat-bread known for beautiful brown blisters, bubbles, and airiness. Across Asia and India, naan is baked at high temperatures in a tandoor (or cylindrical clay oven). Unless you own a tandoor, I recommend using a cast-iron skillet to cook the naan. (A frying pan or heavy skillet will do too.) Naan dough is usually leavened with yeast. Here we'll use sourdough starter,

which results in an airy, soft, and tender sourdough naan bread with a subtle tang and herbaceousness thanks to fresh basil.

SAB member Melissa Duchan posted a mouthwatering picture of her sourdough starter naan and shared a recipe found in thegingeredwhisk.com, which is adapted here.

RECIPE SPECS

FOR THE NAAN

8 ounces (227 g)
100 percent hydration
sourdough starter, unfed

½ cup (120 g)
warm milk

¼ cup (60 g) plain
Greek yogurt

2 cups (250 g)
all-purpose flour

½ teaspoon baking
powder

1 teaspoon
granulated sugar

1 teaspoon miso

½ cup (20 g) fresh
basil, finely chopped

¼ cup (60 g) melted
ghee or butter

**FOR THE OPTIONAL
TOPPINGS**

¼ cup (15 g) fresh
parsley, minced

Sea salt flakes

1 In a stand mixer fitted with the dough hook attachment, mix the sourdough starter, warm milk, and yogurt until combined. Sift in the flour, baking powder, and sugar. Add the miso and basil. Mix until a shaggy, tacky dough forms.

2 Cover and let rise for a few hours, until roughly doubled in size. Do the poke test. Oil a clean finger and poke the dough. If the dough springs back, it's ready.

3 If you're not ready to make the naan yet, refrigerate the dough until you're ready, for up to 12 hours.

4 Preheat a greased cast-iron skillet or frying pan over medium heat.

5 Transfer the dough to a floured work surface. Flour your hands and knead the dough until smooth. Divide the dough into eight even pieces, roughly 80 g (3 ounces) each. Use a rolling pin to roll each piece into an oval about ⅛ to ¼ inch (4 to 6 mm) thick, depending on how thick you prefer your naan to be. If the dough is too tacky and sticky, rub flour over the rolling pin. Brush one side of each piece with the melted ghee or butter. Place a piece of dough, butter-side down, on the skillet and cook for 1 minute, until you see bubbles. Brush the top with the melted ghee or butter. Flip and cook for another minute, until brown blisters appear. Transfer to a serving plate and sprinkle with the optional fresh minced parsley and sea salt flakes. Repeat the steps to cook the remaining pieces of dough.

6 Enjoy with curry, hummus, or just plain. Wrap leftover naan in aluminum foil and refrigerate for up to 3 days. Reheat the naan in the aluminum foil in the oven at 350°F (180°C, or gas mark 4) for about 10 minutes.

To learn how to make a sourdough starter, please visit modernasianbaking.com. You can also buy one online, see if a neighbor can give you one, or check with your local artisan bakers to see if they have starters for sale.

PREP TIME	15 MINUTES
INACTIVE TIME	2 TO 4 HOURS
COOK TIME	10 MINUTES
YIELD	8 PIECES

There's great joy in eating naan the traditional way, with your hands, tearing chunks of it to use as a vessel for delicious gravies and curries.

To change up your curry fillings, try adding minced seitan or another protein, like half a seasoned chicken breast (diced) as recipe testers Ingrid and Sabrina Koo recommend.

Japanese Curry Bread Buns

Japanese Curry Bread Buns (or *kare pan*) are the ultimate comfort food. I love how crispy and crunchy these buns are thanks to the panko coating. They go down fast, so feel free to double the ingredients to make eight buns instead of four.

This recipe is adapted from one found on SAB by Herman Huang (@hnckitchen on Instagram).

FOR THE CURRY BREAD DOUGH

¾ cup plus 3 table-spoons (128 g) bread flour, sifted

½ teaspoon instant yeast

1 tablespoon (8 g) tapioca flour

1 teaspoon granulated sugar

Pinch of salt

⅓ cup plus 2 table-spoons (108 g) milk

1 tablespoon (14 g) butter, room temperature

FOR THE CURRY FILLING

1 tablespoon (14 g) butter

⅓ cup (55 g) diced onion

2 garlic cloves, minced

½ cup (65 g) diced carrot

About ½ cup (65 g) diced potatoes

1 teaspoon miso

1 tablespoon (6 g) curry powder

½ to 1 teaspoon soy sauce, adjust to taste

½ teaspoon brown sugar

3 tablespoons (45 g) water

¼ cup (60 g) coconut milk

Pinch of salt, or to taste

FOR THE CORNSTARCH SLURRY

2 teaspoons cornstarch

4 tablespoons (60 g) water

FOR THE EGG WASH AND CRUMB COATING

1 egg (about 2 ounces, or 50 g), beaten

Panko mixed with a pinch of salt

PREP TIME	35 MINUTES
INACTIVE TIME	ABOUT 60 MINUTES
COOK TIME	ABOUT 60 MINUTES
YIELD	4 BUNS

1 *Make the curry bread dough.* In a large bowl, sift together all the dry ingredients. Add the milk and butter and mix with a flexible spatula or chopsticks until a dough forms. Drizzle in a little milk if the dough is too dry. Knead until soft and smooth. Cover and let rise until roughly doubled in size, about 45 minutes.

2 *Make the curry filling.* In a heavy saucepan, add the butter, onions, and garlic and sauté over medium heat until aromatic. Add the rest of the curry filling ingredients. Cook until the vegetables soften, occasionally stirring the mixture.

3 *Make the cornstarch slurry.* In a small bowl, dissolve the cornstarch in the water. Add the cornstarch slurry to the saucepan. Mix and cook until the slurry thickens. Remove from heat, cover, and cool until it's okay to touch, about 10 minutes.

4 Line a large baking sheet with parchment paper.

5 Deflate the dough. Divide into four equal pieces. Roll each piece into a ball. Use a floured rolling pin to roll into a disc about 6 inches (15 cm) in diameter.

6 Add 2 to 3 tablespoons (30 to 45 g) of curry filling to the middle of the dough disc, keeping the edges of the disc clean. Wet the edges with dabs of water. Fold the disc in half. Pinch the edges together tightly to seal. Take the seam edge and fold down (like sealing a letter). Pinch to seal again. Transfer the bun seam-side down to the baking sheet. Repeat to make three more curry bread buns.

7 Cover and proof for 20 minutes.

8 Coat each bun with the egg wash. Combine the panko and salt in a large dish. Dip and roll each bun until thoroughly coated.

9 Fill a heavy saucepan with about 3 inches (7.5 cm) of neutral oil. Once the oil reaches 325°F (170°C), place the buns seam-side down in the oil. This will cook and seal the seam first and prevent the fillings from bursting out. A few seconds after adding the buns to the oil, use tongs or chopsticks to carefully rotate the buns. Fry over medium-low heat until the buns float up and are thoroughly golden brown.

10 Remove with a slotted spoon; drain on absorbent paper. Enjoy the crunch!

Korean Garlicky Cream Cheese Milk Bread Buns

Warning: These decadent buns are anything but guilt-free. But it's okay to indulge every now and then—like on days when nothing's going right. We all have those days. I'm having one of those days now as I'm writing this recipe. This popular Korean street food will cheer you up and comfort you. It has certainly cheered me up! It's crispy and crunchy on the outside and soft, luscious, and creamy on the inside. To sum up this bread in one word: heavenly. Hashtag #mentalhealthawareness

Note: If you're short on time, feel free to use store-bought buns.

This recipe is inspired by many found on SAB, particularly one by Ranjan Thapa (@foodandstuff101 on Instagram).

FOR THE BREAD

1 recipe Super Easy
Milk Bread dough (see
page 100)

1 egg (about 2 ounces,
or 50 g), beaten, for
egg wash

FOR THE FILLING

12 ounces (338 g) cream
cheese, softened

1½ tablespoons (30 g)
sweetened condensed
milk, adjust to taste

2 garlic cloves, minced

½ teaspoon miso
(optional)

FOR THE GARLICKY
BUTTER SAUCE

½ cup (1 stick, or 112 g)
butter, melted

8 to 10 garlic cloves,
minced

1 egg (about 2 ounces,
or 50 g), beaten

1 tablespoon (4 g)
parsley, chopped

2 scallions, minced

1 tablespoon (20 g)
honey

1 tablespoon (19 g)
sweetened
condensed milk

Dash of garlic powder
(optional)

Dash of paprika
(optional)

FOR THE OPTIONAL
TOPPINGS

2 tablespoons (14 g)
panko

Sea salt flakes

1 Line a large baking sheet with parchment paper.

2 *Make the milk bread dough,* cover, and let rise for 60 minutes, until roughly doubled in size. Deflate and transfer to a floured work surface. Divide into four to six even pieces. Shape each piece into a smooth ball (see technique on page 21). Transfer the dough balls to the prepared baking sheet, cover, and proof for 60 minutes, until roughly doubled in size.

3 About 30 minutes before you're ready to bake the buns, preheat the oven to 350°F (180°C, or gas mark 4) and place a rack in the center.

4 *Make the filling.* Mix the cream cheese, condensed milk, garlic, and optional miso together. Transfer the cream cheese mixture into a piping bag and set aside.

5 *Make the garlicky sauce.* Mix the melted butter, garlic, egg, parsley, scallions, honey, condensed milk, and optional garlic powder and paprika together.

6 Use a pastry brush to lightly brush the buns with the egg wash. Bake for 20 minutes, remove from the oven, and cool completely. Keep the oven running.

7 Make four cuts on the top of each bun (halfway down) to make eight even wedges. Do not cut through the bread. Carefully pipe the filling between each wedge of each bun. Dip the top of each bun into the garlicky sauce. Top the buns with the optional panko and sea salt flakes.

8 Bake the sauced-up buns again for 10 minutes at 350°F (180°C, or gas mark 4), until crispy. Enjoy them hot!

PREP TIME	20 MINUTES
INACTIVE TIME	2 HOURS
COOK TIME	30 MINUTES
YIELD	4 TO 6 BUNS

You can replace the butter with vegan butter for the miso garlic butter spread.

Miso Garlic Milk Bread Buns

When I have spare time and find myself craving something buttery, garlicky, and super satisfying, I bake a batch of these buns to share with my seven-year-old foodie, Philip, who once exclaimed, "Mom, these are the best buns ever!"

FOR THE BUNS

1 recipe Super Easy Milk Bread dough (see page 100)

FOR THE MISO GARLIC BUTTER

½ cup (1 stick, or 112 g) butter, softened

1 heaping tablespoon (16 g) miso

Dash of salt, pepper, and paprika, to taste

4 garlic cloves, minced

2 scallions, minced

½ teaspoon garlic powder (optional)

½ teaspoon bouillon powder (optional)

Minced chives and parsley, to taste (optional)

FOR THE OPTIONAL EGG WASH

1 egg (about 2 ounces, or 50 g), beaten

1 *Make the milk bread dough.* Let rise in an oiled bowl for 60 minutes, until roughly doubled in size.

2 Generously grease or line an 8 x 8-inch (20.5 x 20.5 cm) baking pan with parchment paper that overhangs all sides.

3 *Make the miso garlic butter.* Mix all the miso garlic butter ingredients in a bowl until incorporated. Go ahead and taste it! If needed, heat the butter mixture in the microwave on high in 10-second bursts, until easily spreadable.

4 Deflate the dough. Transfer to a floured work surface. Roll the dough into a long rectangle about 13 x 9 inches (33 x 23 cm), while maintaining an even thickness.

5 Spread the butter mixture evenly over the dough. Leave about 1 to 2 tablespoons (14 to 28 g) of butter mixture for later. Roll the dough into a jelly roll. With the seam-side down, slice into nine even 1 inch (2.5 cm) portions.

6 Place all the buns, cut-side up, on the prepared pan in a three-by-three array. Proof for 60 minutes, until roughly doubled in size.

7 About 25 minutes before you're ready to bake, preheat the oven to 350°F (180°C, or gas mark 4) and place a rack in the center. Brush the optional egg wash evenly over the buns. Bake for 30 to 40 minutes, until the tops are golden brown and a heavenly, garlicky, buttery scent fills your kitchen. About 15 minutes into baking, cover the bread with a sheet of aluminum foil.

8 Remove from the oven. Spread the remaining butter over the tops of the buns. Let the buns cool on the pan for 10 minutes before cooling on a wire rack. I like these buns piping hot!

PREP TIME	**15 MINUTES**
INACTIVE TIME	**120 MINUTES**
COOK TIME	**30 TO 40 MINUTES**
YIELD	**9 BUNS**

No-Knead
Miso Focaccia

This crispy yet chewy focaccia is as umamiful as it is impressive. It's also ridiculously easy to make. Other than time, it *kneads* little else from us bakers.

This recipe is inspired by one found on SAB by George Lee (@chez.jorge on Instagram). George equates fresh-out-of-the-oven focaccia to a warm, loving embrace. I can't agree more!

Note: SAB member Anthea Tang tested this recipe and wants you to know if you want these buns for, let's say, lunchtime on Saturday, then start making them Friday morning.

RECIPE SPECS

FOR THE FOCACCIA

2 cups (250 g) all-purpose flour

About 2 cups (275 g) bread flour

1½ heaping tablespoons (24 g) miso

5 garlic cloves, minced (optional)

12 fluid ounces (355 g) warm water (around 110°F, 43°C)

1 packet (2¼ teaspoons, or 7 to 8 g) active dry yeast

1 tablespoon (20 g) honey

High-quality extra-virgin olive oil, for drizzling and greasing the pan (keep the bottle nearby)

1 tablespoon (15 g) sesame oil (optional)

FOR THE OPTIONAL TOPPINGS

2 scallions

1 teaspoon toasted sesame seeds

4 cherry tomatoes, sliced into halves

1 shallot, cut crosswise into full rings

Toasted sesame seeds for sprinkling

1 *Make the dough.* In a large bowl, combine the all-purpose flour, bread flour, miso, and optional garlic. In a separate bowl, combine the warm water, yeast, and honey. Set aside for 10 minutes. If you see foams and bubbles, the yeast is alive. Add the yeast mixture to the flour. Using a flexible spatula, thoroughly mix until well incorporated and a dough forms. Brush a tablespoon (15 g) of olive oil over the entire surface of the dough. Cover and rest for 30 minutes.

2 Wet your hands. To stretch and fold the dough, take one corner of the dough, stretch it up high (vertically) without tearing, and fold it over the dough. Rotate the bowl 90 degrees and take another corner and repeat. Continue to do this for about 3 minutes. Then cover and refrigerate for 18 to 24 hours.

3 Generously grease a 9 x 13-inch (23 x 33 cm) baking pan with about 2 tablespoons (30 g) of olive oil. Rest the dough at room temperature for 10 minutes. Turn the dough out onto the pan. With clean hands, press and spread out the dough evenly into all four corners of the pan. Cover and proof until puffy, about 2 to 4 hours.

4 About 30 minutes before baking, preheat the oven to 425°F (220°C, or gas mark 7) and place a rack in the center. Apply about 2 tablespoons (30 g) olive oil to the dough. Finger-stipple the entire dough (without tearing) to make divots for the olive oil.

5 Drizzle the optional sesame oil. Decorate with the optional toppings of choice.

6 Bake for 25 to 28 minutes, until lightly golden brown and crispy on top. Remove from the oven and cool on a wire rack. Slice into even strips. Lightly sprinkle with sea salt flakes and serve warm.

If you'd like to spice things up, try adding a little chili crisp oil (instead of sesame oil) to the dough prior to baking. Skip the honey for a vegan focaccia.

PREP TIME	**20 MINUTES**
INACTIVE TIME	**ABOUT 28 HOURS**
COOK TIME	**25 TO 28 MINUTES**
YIELD	**ONE 9 X 13-INCH (23 X 33 CM) FOCACCIA BREAD**

Treats Under
One Moon and
Holiday Bakes

To me, the moon will always hold a lot of significance. When my family and I celebrate the Mid-Autumn Festival and Winter Solstice Festival, we admire the full moon while enjoying moon-cakes (page 128) and *tangyuan* (page 126).

Food and treats are at the heart of our celebrations as they connect us and are meant to be shared. Some recipes here, such as the Mochi Waffle Holiday Tree (page 138) and Hidden Surprise Jade Madeleines (page 124), are perfect for the holidays and celebrations. Other recipes here are suitable for any occasion. Take my Hong Kong Dan Tat (page 120), for example. It was Dad's favorite snack and dim sum. Beloved by many for its silky, eggy filling and buttery crust, egg tarts (or *dan tat*) are always crave-worthy and satisfying all year round. It's definitely a treat worth celebrating.

Near or far, together or apart, I'm always comforted knowing my loved ones, friends, and I are always under one moon. We'll always have all these delicious dishes to connect us. I'm so happy to share these recipes with you, my dear friend. May you find joy and happiness always as you make these dishes and enjoy them with your loved ones.

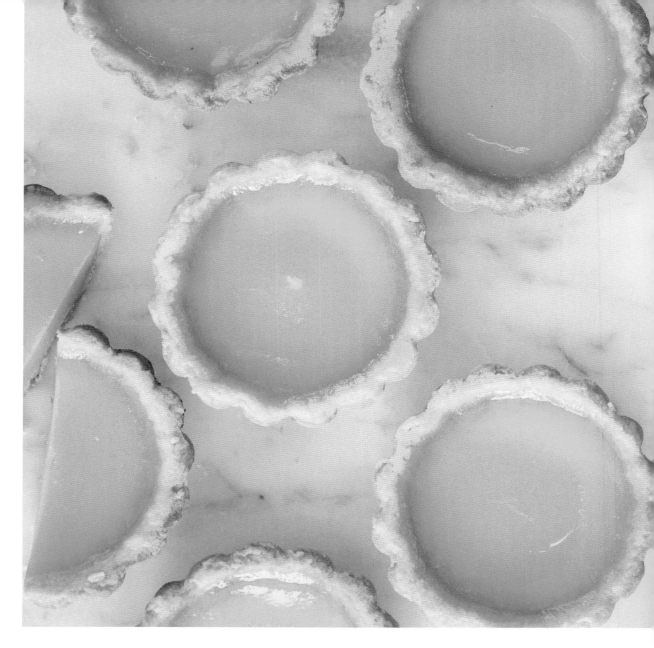

Hong Kong Dan Tat

At the end of dim sum, Dad always had room for a Hong Kong egg tart (or *dan tat*). The warm and inviting combination of silky egg custard and buttery yet light pastry tart must have been super comforting to him.

This recipe is adapted from one found on thewoksoflife.com, an Asian culinary website run by a family of four cooks, admired around the world by SAB members (including myself).

Note: Please have tart molds, tarts tins, or a nonstick muffin pan ready.

FOR THE PASTRY CRUST

2 cups (250 g) all-purpose flour, sifted

⅓ cup (40 g) confectioners' sugar, sifted

¾ cup (1½ sticks, or 165 g) butter, cold

1 teaspoon miso

About 3 tablespoons (44 g) milk

FOR THE CUSTARD FILLING

1 cup (235 g) warm water or milk

⅜ cup (85 g) granulated sugar

4 medium eggs (about 7 ounces, or 200 g), room temperature, beaten

¼ cup (60 g) evaporated milk

1 teaspoon vanilla extract

Pinch of salt

1 *Make the pastry crust.* In a large bowl, combine the flour and sugar. Using a pastry cutter or fork, chop the butter into the dry ingredients until you have pea-sized fragments that are well distributed. Alternatively, hand rub and pinch the butter into the flour. The resulting butter fragments do not all have to be the same size, just no bigger than peas. Add the miso and milk and form a shaggy dough. If the dough appears too dry and crumbly, mix in a little more milk, about ½ teaspoon at a time. Cover and refrigerate for 30 minutes.

2 Place the dough on top of a large sheet of plastic wrap. With a floured rolling pin, roll the dough into a rectangle about 8 x 13 inches (20.5 x 33 cm).

3 Use the plastic wrap to help fold the bottom third of the pastry up into the middle third and then fold the top third down and over the top (like folding a letter). Flip the pastry, seam-side-down, and rotate it 90 degrees so the short edge is facing you.

4 Roll the dough again into a rectangle about 8 x 13 inches (20.5 x 33 cm). Fold into thirds again. Cover and refrigerate for at least 60 minutes.

5 About 30 minutes before baking, preheat the oven to 350°F (180°C, or gas mark 4) and place a rack in the lower third.

6 *Make the custard filling.* In a large bowl, mix the warm water and sugar until all the sugar dissolves. Add the eggs and whisk until incorporated. Add the evaporated milk, vanilla extract, and salt and whisk until combined and smooth. Sieve the mixture through a fine-mesh strainer, cover, and set aside.

7 Remove the pastry dough from the refrigerator. Transfer to a lightly floured work surface. Roll the dough out into a ⅛ inch (3 mm)-thick rectangle. Use a 4-inch (10 cm) cookie cutter (or a fluted or scalloped cookie cutter, as recipe tester Sharon Yeung suggests) to make about twelve tart shells. You may need to re-roll the dough to make all twelve. Fit and mold each tart shell into greased tart molds, tarts tins, or nonstick muffin pans.

8 Add the custard filling to each tart shell so all are about 75 percent full.

9 Bake for about 25 minutes, until the edges of the crust are golden brown and the filling is not runny.

10 Serve warm. Refrigerate leftovers in an airtight container for up to 3 days. Reheat in the oven at 350°F (180°C, or gas mark 4) for 10 minutes.

PREP TIME	30 MINUTES
COOK TIME	30 MINUTES
YIELD	ABOUT 12 DAN TAT

To make mango roses, peel and slice a mango in half. Slice, lengthwise, into thin pieces. Coil one piece tightly. This will be the center of the "rose." Wrap a second piece, a "petal," around the center. Continue to add pieces of "petals," working your way outward.

SAB Bake-Off Summer Fruit Tart

SAB's first global bake-off theme was summer fruit tart. One of the winning entries was an unforgettable and beautiful mango, fig, and cardamom fruit tart invented by twin sisters Melodie and Justine Deisher (@betwin_the_lines on Instagram). This recipe is an adaptation of their stunning dessert.

Note: You'll need some uncooked rice or dried beans when blind-baking the short crust pastry.

FOR THE SHORT CRUST PASTRY

½ cup (1 stick) plus 2 tablespoons (140 g) butter, softened

⅓ cup (67 g) granulated sugar

1 egg (about 2 ounces, or 50 g)

Pinch of salt

2 cups (250 g) all-purpose flour, sifted

About ¼ cup (36 g) unsalted pistachios or pine nuts, pulsed in a food processor

FOR THE CRÈME PÂTISSIÈRE (OR PASTRY CREAM)

1 cup plus 1 tablespoon (250 g) milk

3 egg yolks (about 2 ounces, or 60 g)

⅓ cup (67 g) granulated sugar

1 tablespoon (8 g) cornstarch

2 tablespoons (16 g) all-purpose flour

¼ teaspoon cardamom

¼ teaspoon nutmeg (optional)

1 teaspoon vanilla extract (optional)

Pinch of salt

FOR THE TOPPINGS

1 to 2 ripe mangos, chilled and thinly sliced (to make mango roses)

Mint leaves (optional)

Fresh figs (optional)

Edible gold flakes (optional)

1 Lightly grease and flour a 9- or 9½-inch (23 or 24 cm) nonstick tart tin.

2 *Make the short crust pastry.* In a stand mixer fitted with the paddle attachment, cream the butter and sugar until combined. Add the egg and salt and mix on low speed until incorporated, scraping down the sides of the bowl as needed. Fold the flour and nuts into the mixture until just combined, without overworking the dough. Shape the dough into a ball. Cover and refrigerate for 30 minutes.

3 On a lightly floured work surface, roll the pastry into a disc slightly larger than the tart tin. Carefully drape the pastry over the tart tin. Gently mold the dough into the tin, until flush against the tin all the way around. Run a knife around the edge of the tart tin to cut away excess dough. (You can freeze the excess dough and thaw it when ready to use for smaller tarts.) Using a fork, poke holes across the surface of the dough. Cover and refrigerate for at least 15 minutes.

4 Preheat the oven to 350°F (180°C, or gas mark 4) and place a rack in the center.

5 *Make the crème pâtissière.* In a heavy saucepan over medium-low heat, bring the milk to a boil. Set aside. In a large bowl, whisk to combine the remaining crème pâtissière ingredients. Gradually pour the hot milk into the bowl and whisk until fully incorporated.

6 Heat the mixture in the saucepan over medium heat, whisking constantly until it thickens into a smooth and creamy pudding consistency. Remove from heat, whisk to help it cool, and transfer to a bowl. Cover with plastic wrap, with the wrap clinging to the surface of the crème pâtissière. Refrigerate for at least 1 hour.

7 Meanwhile, line the short crust pastry with parchment paper and fill with uncooked rice. Bake for about 25 to 30 minutes, until golden brown. Remove the parchment paper and rice and bake the pastry for an additional 5 minutes. Cool completely.

8 *Assemble the tart.* Fill the tart shell with the crème pâtissière. Smooth the surface with a pastry scraper or icing spatula. Decorate and garnish the tart with mango roses and your choice of toppings.

PREP TIME	30 MINUTES
COOK TIME	35 MINUTES
YIELD	ONE 9-INCH (23 CM) TART

For the best-looking chocolate shells, use silicone madeleine molds.

Hidden Surprise Jade Madeleines

During the holidays, these lovely jade matcha-infused bites are perfect as gifts. Be as creative as you desire when adding your surprise ingredient to each madeleine. Just be sure the ingredient, such as nuts or candied ginger, bakes well. A candy thermometer will come in handy for this recipe.

This recipe was adapted from one by James Campbell, author of *Japanese Patisserie*. A post on SAB by Megan Pham (@takestwoeggs on Instagram) inspired the addition of the beautiful white chocolate matcha shells.

RECIPE SPECS

FOR THE MADELEINES

About 6 tablespoons (50 g) all-purpose flour, sifted

About ½ cup (50 g) almond flour, sifted

1 tablespoon (6 g) matcha

½ teaspoon baking powder

Pinch of salt

Pinch of cardamom (optional)

About ½ cup (1 stick) plus 2 tablespoons (150 g) butter, diced

3 medium eggs (about 5 ounces, or 150 g), room temperature

⅓ cup (67 g) granulated sugar

FOR THE SURPRISES

12 individual surprises of choice, such as dried berries, candied ginger, or nuts

FOR THE CHOCOLATE SHELL

⅔ cup (100 g) ivory-colored white chocolate (made with cocoa butter), chopped

1 tablespoon (14 g) salted or unsalted butter

2 teaspoons matcha

Pinch of salt

Edible rose petals or gold leaf for garnishing (optional)

1 *Make the madeleine batter.* In a bowl, sift together the flours, matcha, baking powder, salt, and optional cardamom and set aside.

2 In a saucepan over medium heat, melt and boil the butter until the fat at the bottom of the pan is nut-brown (but not too dark), about 8 to 9 minutes. Pour the browned butter into a heatproof bowl. Let cool to about 98°F (37°C), checking with a candy thermometer.

3 In a stand mixer fitted with the whisk attachment, beat the eggs and sugar on medium-high speed until pale in color and thick, about 8 minutes. The whisk should leave trails in the batter. Gradually add the dry ingredients and brown butter to the egg mixture, gently folding each time to incorporate the ingredients. *Be patient. Do not stir or whisk.* The final batter should be shiny, smooth, and not lumpy. Cover and refrigerate for at least an hour, preferably overnight. The batter will thicken.

4 About 30 minutes before baking, preheat the oven to 445°F (230°C, or gas mark 8) and place a rack in the center.

5 Generously grease a 12-cavity scalloped madeleine mold. Lightly sprinkle flour on each mold. Spoon the batter into the cavities, about three-fourths of the way full. Press a surprise filling of choice into the center of each madeleine. Bake for 2 minutes. Lower the temperature to 350°F (180°C, or gas mark 4) and bake for 10 to 12 minutes, until risen and golden brownish-green. Remove from the oven and allow the madeleines to set in the mold for a few minutes before removing.

6 In a microwave-safe bowl, heat the white chocolate and butter in the microwave, in 15-second bursts, stirring after each burst, until melted and smooth. Add the matcha and salt and mix until smooth and incorporated. Pipe or spoon the matcha chocolate to line each cavity of the madeleine mold.

7 Place the madeleines on top of the matcha chocolate. Allow the chocolate to set at room temperature or in the refrigerator for at least 15 minutes.

8 Garnish with rose petals or gold leaf, if desired. Madeleines taste best the day they're baked. Refrigerate any leftover madeleine batter and use within 3 days.

PREP TIME	20 MINUTES
INACTIVE TIME	1 HOUR TO OVERNIGHT
COOK TIME	25 MINUTES
YIELD	12 MADELEINES, DEPENDING ON THE SIZE OF THE MOLDS

Switch up the flavor of the filling by substituting the matcha with black sesame powder.

Heartwarming Lava Tangyuan

Ever since the Song Dynasty, during the Winter Solstice, families would make and eat *tangyuan* (soup ball) together, as tangyuan symbolizes harmony and togetherness. Here we fill tangyuan with matcha chocolate that oozes like verdant lava when hot. Bet you this dish can warm even the Grinch's heart.

This recipe is inspired by one found on SAB by Regina Ip (@pigoutyvr on Instagram).

Note: This recipe requires patience and practice.

**FOR THE MATCHA
LAVA FILLING**

1 tablespoon (15 g)
heavy cream

2 tablespoons (28 g)
butter

About ⅓ cup (55 g)
ivory-colored white
chocolate (made with
cocoa butter), chopped

1 teaspoon
vanilla extract

Pinch of salt

1 to 2 teaspoons matcha,
adjust to taste

**FOR THE TANGYUAN
WRAPPER**

About 1 cup plus
1 tablespoon (130 g)
glutinous rice flour

3 tablespoons (24 g)
confectioners' sugar

Pinch of salt

¼ cup (60 g)
boiling water

1 teaspoon neutral oil

¼ cup (60 g)
cold water

FOR THE SWEET SOUP

2 cups (475 g) water

About ½ cup
(120 g) packed dark
brown sugar

6 jujubes, sliced

A handful of dried
goji berries

1 teaspoon matcha
(optional)

PREP TIME	30 MINUTES
COOK TIME	10 MINUTES
YIELD	12 TANGYUAN BALLS

1 *Make the matcha lava filling.* In a small saucepan, heat all the filling ingredients over low heat while whisking continuously, just until all the chocolate and butter melt. Remove from heat. Transfer to a small baking tray or dish, cover, and freeze for at least 45 minutes, until solid.

2 *Make the tangyuan wrapper.* In a large bowl, combine the glutinous rice flour, sugar, salt, hot water, and oil. Mix until floury pebbles form. Add the cold water and mix until incorporated. Dust your hands with glutinous rice flour and knead the dough. If the dough is too wet and sticky, add glutinous rice flour, a teaspoon at a time. If it is too dry, add a little water. Knead until smooth. Pinch off three 15 g (about ½ ounce) pieces of dough and shape into balls. Cook the balls in boiling water until they float, about 5 minutes. Toss them back into the uncooked dough. When cool enough to touch, knead and stretch until fully incorporated. At this point, if the dough doesn't seem very pliable, mix in a teaspoon of oil.

3 Divide the dough into twelve even portions about 20 g (¾ ounce) each and form them into balls. Cover.

4 *Assemble the tangyuan.* Remove the filling from the freezer. Roll a piece of dough into a disc about 2 inches (5 cm) in diameter. The disc should not be too thin, and the middle should be thicker than the edges. Spoon a portion of filling (about 6 to 7 g, or ¼ ounce) and shape into a ball. Place the filling in the middle of the dough disc. Close the disc over the filling and pinch the seam shut. Roll in your hand into a smooth, round ball. Repeat to make eleven more.

5 *Make the sweet soup.* Boil the water in a heavy saucepan and reduce the heat to low. Add the rest of the sweet soup ingredients and stir to incorporate. Remove from heat, cover, and set aside.

6 Bring a large pot filled about halfway with water to boil. Add the tangyuan and stir while cooking over medium-high heat. Once the water boils again, add a cup (235 g) of water to the pot. When the tangyuan all float to the surface, cook for 1 more minute. Remove from the pot with a slotted spoon and transfer to the saucepan with the sweet soup.

7 Divide the tangyuan and sweet soup among two to four bowls. Enjoy them hot.

Snowy Skin Mooncake

With this fun and customizable recipe, we can make and enjoy beautiful Snowy Skin Mooncakes of any color, any day, and not just during the Mid-Autumn Festival. Start with the salted egg yolk custard filling. Then try a different filling, such as ube halaya jam (page 28).

This recipe is adapted from one found on SAB by Karen Ng (@hustle_ng on Instagram).

Notes: You will need a 50 to 100 g (1¼ to 3½ ounce) capacity mooncake mold press, which is inexpensive and easy to find online. This recipe uses cooked salted duck egg yolks that are easily found in the frozen or refrigerated section of Asian markets or online in vacuum-sealed packages.

FOR THE TOASTED GLUTINOUS RICE FLOUR

About 4 tablespoons (32 g) glutinous rice flour

FOR THE FILLING

3 tablespoons (45 g) melted butter

½ cup (120 g) milk

6 tablespoons (78 g) granulated sugar, adjust to taste

3 medium eggs (about 5 ounces, or 150 g), beaten

1 teaspoon vanilla extract

1 to 2 salted duck egg yolks (½ to 1 ounce, or 14 to 28 g), steamed for 15 minutes and then mashed with a fork

¼ teaspoon miso or salt

4 tablespoons (32 g) cornstarch

3 tablespoons (36 g) custard powder, sifted (optional)

FOR THE MOONCAKE SKIN

½ cup (60 g) glutinous rice flour

¼ cup (40 g) rice flour

3 tablespoons (24 g) cornstarch

3 tablespoons (39 g) granulated sugar

¾ cup plus 2 teaspoons (185 g) milk

About 1½ tablespoons (25 g) sweetened condensed milk

2 tablespoons (30 g) canola oil (or other neutral oil), plus more for brushing

1 teaspoon vanilla extract (optional)

A few drops food coloring gel; color of your choice (optional)

FOR THE OPTIONAL DECORATION

Edible gold dust or gold flakes

PREP TIME	45 MINUTES
COOK TIME	40 MINUTES
YIELD	ABOUT 15 MOONCAKES

1 *Make the toasted glutinous rice flour.* In a pan over medium-low heat, toast the flour until aromatic. Set aside.

2 *Make the filling.* In a saucepan, add all the filling ingredients and whisk until fully combined. Heat over medium-low heat while continuously whisking. When the mixture thickens, pulls away from the saucepan, and balls up, remove from heat. Smooth out the filling with a flexible spatula. It's okay for the filling to be a bit lumpy. Cover with plastic wrap touching the filling. Refrigerate for at least an hour.

3 *Make the mooncake skin.* Add all the mooncake skin ingredients to a heatproof bowl and whisk until smooth and homogeneous. Cover the bowl with aluminum foil. Steam for at least 30 minutes over medium-high heat, until the mixture solidifies and is not runny (see technique on page 17). The mochi dough is ready when it resembles a stiff jelly and an inserted toothpick (or bamboo stick) comes out clean.

4 Transfer the dough to a stand mixer fitted with the paddle attachment. Mix on low speed until shiny and smooth, 1 to 2 minutes. Do not overwork the dough.

5 Allow the dough to cool to the touch.

6 *Assemble the mooncakes.* Wear food-safe gloves. If desired, add drops of food coloring to the mochi dough. Stretch and mix until the dough is marbled with the food coloring. Scoop a heaping tablespoon (about 20 g) of dough. Roll into a ball and flatten it between two layers of plastic wrap. Remove from the plastic wrap. Take a large tablespoon (about 25 g) of filling and roll into a ball. Wrap the dough around the filling, pinch in the seams, and roll into a smooth ball. Toss the ball around in the pan with the toasted glutinous flour. Dust the inside of the mooncake mold press with the toasted glutinous rice flour. Use the press (with the stamp of choice) to gently stamp down on the dusted ball to complete the mooncake. Repeat to make about fourteen more mooncakes. Brush with neutral oil. Decorate with gold dust or gold flakes, if desired.

7 Cover and refrigerate for a few hours and up to 4 days. Allow the mooncakes to soften at room temperature before enjoying.

Lunar
New Year
Nian Gao

Nian gao (sweet rice cake) is an auspicious food like many other foods eaten during Lunar New Year. *Nian* means year. While *gao* means cake in Cantonese, it's also a homonym for tall or high; thus, nian gao symbolizes a good, prosperous year ahead. Without fail, my mother would serve us pan-fried nian gao for breakfast every morning on the first day of Lunar New Year.

I never gave our traditions much thought or appreciated this simple QQ and not-too-sweet cake until I moved away from New York City and stopped having nian gao during Lunar New Year for a few years. These days, I make sure we have plenty of nian gao and other foods that symbolize good luck and fortune to go around every Lunar New Year.

RECIPE SPECS

FOR THE NIAN GAO

1 cup (235 g) hot water

½ cup (115 g) packed dark brown sugar

¼ teaspoon salt

2 cups (240 g) glutinous rice flour, sifted

¼ cup (60 g) coconut cream from a chilled can of coconut milk

1 teaspoon vanilla extract (optional)

½ teaspoon ginger juice, to taste (optional)

FOR THE OPTIONAL DECORATION

1 to 2 dried jujubes

1 Generously grease an 8-inch (20.5 cm) cake pan or line it with parchment paper. Nestle a strip of parchment paper into the sides of the cake pan to form a collar.

2 In a blender, blend all the nian gao ingredients until you get a smooth batter. Refrigerate for 30 minutes. Alternatively, whisk all the ingredients together until smooth, like thinned-out peanut butter.

3 Pour the batter into the prepared pan. Tap the pan against the counter a few times. Smooth out the top of the cake gently by drawing circles on the surface with a whisk. Cover with aluminum foil.

4 Steam the cake over high heat for 35 minutes (see technique on page 17). If steaming over medium-low to medium heat, it may take 60 minutes or longer to cook. Periodically check the water level of the pot and replenish with hot water as needed. The nian gao is ready when an inserted toothpick (or bamboo stick) comes out clean.

5 Remove the nian gao from the steamer and cool. Place a serving plate on top of the nian gao. Flip the nian gao onto the plate. (If you didn't use parchment paper, run a knife gently along the edges where the nian gao adheres to the pan.) If desired, place the jujubes in the middle as decoration. Cut into even slices and serve.

If you'd like to try fried nian gao, refrigerate the nian gao overnight. When ready to fry, whisk together 1 egg and 1 teaspoon of milk in a medium bowl. Lightly coat eight to ten pieces of sliced nian gao with the egg. Grease a frying pan and fry the nian gao over medium heat for 1 to 2 minutes on each side, until a golden brown layer forms. Cool for a few minutes. Pan-fried nian gao are great for breakfast or as a quick snack.

PREP TIME	15 MINUTES
COOK TIME	30 TO 60 MINUTES
YIELD	ONE 8-INCH (20.5 CM) CAKE

If you don't have homemade ube halaya jam handy, please use a store-bought version.

Mochi-Stuffed Ube Crinkle Cookies

When SAB member Tasha Thach posted a picture of her beautiful ube crinkle cookies using a recipe adapted from one by Kurt Bantilan on his website Cooking with Kurt, I just had to re-create them. The inspiration to include a mochi center came from Peony Bakery in Seattle.

Sugary and crispy on the outside, while the centers are extra soft and QQ thanks to the surprise mochi, these cookies will surely please during the holidays, or any day!

FOR THE MOCHI FILLING

½ cup plus 2 table-
spoons (75 g) glutinous
rice flour

¼ cup (30 g) confec-
tioners' sugar, sifted

½ tablespoon
(4 g) cornstarch

½ cup (120 g) water
(or milk for a creamier
mochi)

½ tablespoon (8 g)
butter, softened

FOR THE COOKIE DOUGH

¼ cup (½ stick, or
55 g) butter, softened

⅓ cup (67 g)
granulated sugar

¼ teaspoon miso

1 teaspoon lemon zest
(optional)

1 egg (about
2 ounces, or 50 g)

About 2 heaping
tablespoons (50 g)
ube halaya jam (see
recipe on page 28)

1 teaspoon ube extract

A few drops of
purple food coloring
gel (optional)

About 1⅓ cups (170 g)
all-purpose flour, sifted

1 teaspoon baking
powder

TO COAT THE DOUGHBALLS

½ cup (60 g)
confectioners' sugar

1 *Make the mochi filling.* Follow the directions on page 24 to make quick microwave mochi, using all the filling ingredients. Do not coat the mochi with any cornstarch. Cover and let cool.

2 *Make the cookie dough.* In a stand mixer fitted with the paddle attachment, cream the butter, sugar, miso, and optional lemon zest until pale in color and fluffy, a few minutes. Scrape the sides of the bowl as needed. Add the egg, ube halaya jam, ube extract, and optional drops of purple food coloring. Mix until incorporated. Tip in the flour and baking powder and mix until just combined. Cover and refrigerate for at least 1 hour or overnight.

3 About 30 minutes before baking, preheat the oven to 350°F (180°C, or gas mark 4) and place a rack in the center. Line two large baking sheets with parchment paper.

4 *Assemble the cookies.* Wear food-safe gloves. Divide the mochi dough into twelve small doughballs, about 10 g (⅓ ounce) each. (Store any leftover mochi in an airtight container and use within 2 days.) If the mochi is too sticky to work with, rub a bit of neutral oil on your gloves. Scoop 1½ tablespoons (about 30 g) of cookie dough. Shape the dough into a ball before flattening into a disc. (Dust with flour if the cookie dough is too wet.) Place a mochi ball in the center of the dough disc. Wrap the cookie dough around the mochi ball, close the seams, and roll into a smooth, firm ball. Toss into the bowl of confectioners' sugar and coat thoroughly. Transfer to a prepared baking sheet. Repeat until you've made a total of twelve mochi-filled and coated dough balls.

5 Leave space between each doughball and bake for about 16 minutes, until the edges have set and browned slightly. The cookie centers should be soft but not runny.

6 Cool on the baking sheet for a few minutes before cooling completely on a wire rack.

Many bakers roll the cookie balls in granulated sugar before coating them with confectioners' sugar to prevent the confectioners' sugar from melting.

PREP TIME	30 MINUTES
COOK TIME	30 MINUTES
YIELD	ABOUT 12 COOKIES

Matcha Holiday Wreath Butter Cookies

Sweeten and brighten someone's day with a tin of these adorable matcha wreath cookies. Feel free to add more miso if you like saltier cookies packed with more umami. As they are, these cookies already pop with flavor, especially if you add the optional spices. The poppy seeds add texture, but feel free to omit them if you want uniformly green cookies.

This recipe is inspired by one found on SAB by Eri Karasawa (@tedukuri_eri on Instagram).

FOR THE COOKIE DOUGH

1 tablespoon (9 g) poppy seeds (optional)

½ cup (1 stick) plus 3 tablespoons (157 g) butter, softened

About 6 tablespoons (75 g) granulated sugar

½ tablespoon (8 g) miso

1 egg (about 2 ounces, or 50 g), beaten

1 teaspoon vanilla extract

¼ teaspoon cinnamon or cardamom (optional)

½ tablespoon (3 g) matcha (matcha lovers, add more)

1 teaspoon baking powder

About 1¼ cups (180 g) cake flour

FOR THE TOPPING

About ¼ cup (45 g) ruby or white chocolate

FOR THE OPTIONAL TOPPINGS

Dried cranberries

Pistachios, chopped

Dried rose petals

Edible gold flakes

1 Line two large baking sheets with parchment paper.

2 If using poppy seeds, soak them in hot milk or water for at least 30 minutes. Strain and set aside. In a stand mixer fitted with the paddle attachment, combine the butter, sugar, and miso and beat on medium-high speed until the mixture is light and fluffy, about 3 minutes. Scrape the butter down the mixer sides as needed. Add the egg, one-third at a time, while mixing until incorporated. Add the vanilla extract, optional spice, and optional poppy seeds. Sift together the matcha and baking powder and then gradually sift in the flour. Continue to mix until a well-incorporated dough forms. If the dough appears too dry and not pipeable, mix in a little milk, a teaspoon at a time.

3 Transfer the dough to a piping bag fitted with an open star tip. Pipe *O*-shaped wreaths, about 2 to 2½ inches (5 to 6.5 cm) in diameter and give them some room to account for spreading.

4 Freeze the piped cookies, uncovered, for about 20 minutes before baking.

5 Preheat the oven to 350°F (180°C, or gas mark 4) and place a rack in the center.

6 Bake for about 12 minutes, until the cookie edges darken slightly.

7 Remove from the oven. Let cool and set on the baking sheets.

8 Melt the chocolate in the microwave in 15-second bursts. Dip the cookies in the chocolate and garnish with the optional ingredients as desired. It's the holidays, so be as fancy as you please. Store the cookies in an airtight container for up to 5 days.

Eri recommends the Ateco 825 piping tip with seven slits.

PREP TIME	20 MINUTES
COOK TIME	ABOUT 12 MINUTES
YIELD	ABOUT 25 COOKIES

To make a walnut version of this cookie, omit the almond extract, use raw walnuts instead of the almond slices for topping, and substitute the almond flour with freshly ground walnut flour.

Buttery Lunar New Year Almond Cookies

Resembling gold coins, these buttery cookies are considered an auspicious food. Although often shared during Lunar New Year, almond cookies are also a staple in Chinese bakeries and restaurants. I love how these cookies are not too sweet and straightforward to make. How they crumble and melt with each bite is so delightful.

This recipe is adapted from one found on SAB by Rachel Lin of assortedeats.com.

RECIPE SPECS

FOR THE COOKIES

About 1 cup (120 g) all-purpose flour

About ½ cup (60 g) almond flour

¼ cup (50 g) granulated sugar

½ teaspoon baking soda

½ cup (1 stick, or 112 g) butter, cold and cubed

1 egg yolk (about ¾ ounce, or 20 g), room temperature

1 tablespoon (16 g) miso

½ teaspoon almond extract

½ teaspoon vanilla extract

FOR THE TOPPINGS

Almonds or almond slices

Sesame seeds (optional)

FOR THE EGG WASH

2 egg yolks (about 1½ ounces, or 40 g), beaten

1 In a large bowl, sift in the flour, almond flour, sugar, and baking soda. Mix to combine.

2 With clean hands, rub and pinch the butter into the dry ingredients to evenly distribute the butter, until the mixture resembles pebbly flour. Add the egg yolk, miso, and the extracts. Mix to combine, just until a cohesive dough forms.

3 Shape the dough into a log, cover with plastic wrap, and refrigerate for at least 60 minutes or up to overnight.

4 About 30 minutes before baking, preheat the oven to 350°F (180°C, or gas mark 4) and place a rack in the center. Line two baking sheets with parchment paper.

5 Cut the dough into twelve equal portions. Shape each portion into a ball. Transfer to the prepared sheets, about six doughballs to a sheet, spaced apart. Flatten each doughball into rounds about 2½ to 3 inches (6.5 to 7.5 cm) in diameter.

6 Add two to three almonds or almond slices to the center of each cookie and press down gently. Sprinkle the optional sesame seeds over the tops of the cookies. With clean fingers, press down on the sesame seeds so they will stick to the dough.

7 Brush each cookie with the egg wash.

8 Bake for about 13 minutes, until the tops are golden and the edges begin to darken.

9 Let the cookies cool on the pan for a few minutes before transferring to a wire rack to cool completely.

10 Store leftover cookies in an airtight container at room temperature for up to 3 days.

PREP TIME	**30 MINUTES**
INACTIVE TIME	**UP TO OVERNIGHT TO CHILL THE COOKIE DOUGH**
COOK TIME	**ABOUT 13 MINUTES**
YIELD	**ABOUT 12 COOKIES**

Mochi Waffle Holiday Tree

Are you looking for a bright and cheery dish that's perfect during the holidays? Stack these thick and chewy pandan mochi waffles to resemble an evergreen tree. Garnish this "tree" as desired and have fun with this quick, easy, and festive recipe. Then surprise a loved one with it!

Recipe testers Ingrid and Sabrina Koo insist you try this miso caramel sauce. In fact, Ingrid feels I should bottle up the sauce and sell it! It's that good!

FOR THE WAFFLE BATTER

3 medium eggs (about 5 ounces, or 150 g)

1 cup (235 g) full-fat coconut milk

6 tablespoons (¾ stick, or 85 g) butter, melted

1 to 2 teaspoons green pandan extract

1 teaspoon instant yeast

1½ cups (180 g) glutinous rice flour

2 tablespoons (16 g) tapioca flour

⅓ cup (67 g) granulated sugar

½ teaspoon baking powder

Pinch of salt

FOR THE MISO CARAMEL SAUCE

½ cup (100 g) granulated sugar

A little less than 1 stick (about ½ cup, or 100 g) butter, cubed

¼ cup (60 g) coconut milk

1 tablespoon (16 g) miso

FOR THE OPTIONAL TOPPINGS

Whipped cream

Fruits of choice

Edible sprinkles

Confectioners' sugar for dusting

1 *Make the waffle batter.* Add all the waffle batter ingredients to a blender, starting with the eggs and other wet ingredients before adding the dry ingredients. Mix on low speed until a smooth batter forms. Cover and refrigerate for 60 minutes.

2 *Make the miso caramel sauce.* Heat the sugar in a heavy saucepan over low heat for about 15 minutes, until melted and caramelized. Add the butter and stir until combined and smooth. Add the coconut milk and continuously whisk as it simmers for about 2 minutes, until the caramel thickens. Add the miso and stir until incorporated. Remove from heat and transfer to a jar. Cover and cool.

3 Preheat the waffle iron or bubble waffle iron. Spray with cooking spray and pour ⅔ cup (about 170 g) of batter (or the amount recommended by the manufacturer) onto the center of the iron. Close the lid and cook for the manufacturer's recommended amount of time until the waffle is golden and cooked thoroughly.

4 Repeat with the remaining batter. Cool completely. Cut the outer rims of the waffles to show off the green interior.

5 *Assemble the waffle holiday tree.* Place one waffle on a serving plate. Cut a second waffle so that it is slightly smaller than the first waffle. Cut a third waffle so it is slightly smaller than the second waffle. Cut the fourth waffle so it is slightly smaller than the third waffle. Stack the waffles on top of each other in size order. Save one to two small pieces of waffle to top the stack.

6 Drizzle the miso caramel sauce over the waffles.

7 Garnish and decorate with your choice of optional toppings. Finally, for a snowy look, dust with confectioners' sugar.

Feel free to replace the miso caramel sauce with syrup or another liquid sweetener.

PREP TIME	20 MINUTES
COOK TIME	30 MINUTES
YIELD	1 WAFFLE HOLIDAY TREE

Custards
and Frozen

Here, you'll find dishes that will keep you cool and refreshed, especially on hot summer days. Only two recipes in this section, the Simply Perfect Purin (page 148) and the Baked Sweet Potato Freezies (page 150), require the use of the oven. The rest of the recipes are non-bake and are mostly enjoyed cold. (The sweet potato freezies can be enjoyed hot or cold.)

Some of the recipes here are even magical, like my Magical Ginger Milk Curd (page 152). Using just fresh ginger juice, milk, and sugar, you'll be making a soft, slippery, and spicy milk pudding. Using milk and gelatin, you'll be making a kawaii Silky Black Sesame Panna Cotta (page 142).

If you've ever had boba tea and wished it were an ice pop, you're in luck because you can make Mochi Boba Milk Tea Ice Pops (page 156) at home. You'll make the boba with glutinous rice flour instead of tapioca flour, as tapioca boba pearls become teeth-cracking hard when frozen.

I truly hope you'll enjoy these recipes and that these dishes will keep you cool and refreshed. They were super fun to create, and I'm so happy to be able to share them with you.

Substitute the black sesame seeds with 1 tablespoon (6 g) of matcha to make matcha panna cotta.

Silky Black Sesame Panna Cotta

Panna cotta means "cooked cream" in Italian. It is usually an egg- and gluten-free dessert that requires no baking. To transform this classic dessert with an Asian twist, I added black sesame seeds and cardamom. The result: an elegant, dark gray dessert that's nutty, creamy, and subtly decadent.

This recipe is inspired by one found on SAB by Emily Lu (@a.e.kitchen_ on Instagram).

RECIPE SPECS

FOR THE PANNA COTTA

About ¼ cup (36 g) black sesame seeds

Sesame oil, or other neutral oil, for brushing

2½ teaspoons (6 g) gelatin

1½ cups (355 g) milk, divided

1 tablespoon (20 g) honey

½ teaspoon cardamom

1 teaspoon glutinous rice flour

1½ cups (355 g) heavy cream, divided

¼ cup (50 g) granulated sugar, to taste

Pinch of salt

1 teaspoon vanilla extract

FOR THE OPTIONAL TOPPINGS

Melted chocolate designs

Berries or other fruits of choice

Whipped cream

Mint leaves

1 In a frying pan over medium heat, toast the black sesame seeds until aromatic, a few minutes. Set aside to cool.

2 Brush the insides of four 8-ounce (235 g) ramekins (or large pudding cups) with sesame or neutral oil.

3 In a bowl, add the gelatin and about one-third of the milk. Stir and let the gelatin bloom (absorb liquid) for a few minutes.

4 In a blender, add the black sesame seeds, honey, cardamom, glutinous rice flour, and the remaining two-thirds of the milk and blend until it resembles gray milk. Scrape down the sides of the blender bowl with a flexible spatula as needed. Add the heavy cream and blend for a few seconds. Use a cheesecloth or fine-mesh strainer to sieve the mixture directly into a heavy saucepan. Mix in the bloomed gelatin, sugar, salt, and vanilla extract. Heat over medium heat while gently stirring the mixture. Once simmering, remove from heat. Use a fine-mesh strainer to sieve directly into the prepared ramekins, dividing evenly among the four. You may have enough to fill a fifth ramekin. If you see excessive foam or bubbles, remove with a spoon. Cover and refrigerate for at least 4 hours.

5 To decorate, pipe melted chocolate shapes and designs directly on parchment paper. When the chocolate design sets, transfer to the panna cotta. (Pictured is a *panda* cotta.)

6 Alternatively, run a knife gently along the edges where the panna cotta adheres to the ramekins and flip out onto serving plates. Add fruits of choice to the plate and dollops of whipped cream to the panna cotta, if desired.

7 Note that the black sesame and cardamom may pool in the bottom of the ramekin.

PREP TIME	20 MINUTES
COOK TIME	10 MINUTES
YIELD	4 PANNA COTTA

Comforting Black Sesame Soup

Having a bowl of this Chinese dessert transports me back to the nineties when my mother was a hardworking home seamstress, always hunched over her sewing machine, even after midnight, struggling to make ends meet. Yet, she still managed to find time to make desserts, such as black sesame soup for our family. "Eat this if you want your hair always to be black and long," she told my sister and me. I'm almost forty, and most of my hair is still black. Black sesame soup is magical indeed.

FOR THE SOUP

⅓ cup (80 g) black sesame powder

⅓ cup (40 g) glutinous rice flour

3 to 4 tablespoons (39 to 52 g) granulated sugar, adjust to taste

½ teaspoon salt

1 teaspoon vanilla extract (optional)

3 cups (705 g) water

1 tablespoon (14 g) butter, softened (optional)

FOR THE OPTIONAL GARNISH

White or black sesame seeds

Edible gold flakes

1 In a frying pan, add the black sesame powder and glutinous rice flour and toast over low heat for 10 minutes, until a nutty aroma fills your kitchen.

2 Add the black sesame powder, flour, sugar, salt, vanilla extract, if using, and water in a blender and mix on high speed until smooth and incorporated.

3 Sieve the mixture through a fine-mesh strainer or cheesecloth. Here we only want the liquid, which results in a smooth and creamier black sesame soup. Heat over medium heat, while continuously whisking, until the black sesame soup thickens to your desired consistency. Stir in the optional butter. Please note that as the mixture cools, it will thicken more.

4 Cool and garnish with the sesame seeds and gold flakes, if desired. Serve warm or chill in the refrigerator for 3 hours or longer to enjoy it cold.

Pulse black sesame seeds in a food processor to make black sesame powder.

PREP TIME	15 MINUTES
COOK TIME	10 TO 20 MINUTES
YIELD	2 BOWLS

No-Churn Corn and Cheese Ice Cream

On a typically muggy New York day, I happened upon a pop-up ice cream stand during my lunch break and got to try corn and cheese ice cream for the first time. I remember how the refreshing ice cream was a perfect marriage of sweet and savory atop a crispy cone. Not to sound *corny*, but I was in love. Soon afterward, I discovered *mais con yelo* and *mais queso* ice cream, two Filipino desserts where cheese and corn are the stars. I made my own version of mais queso (corn cheese) ice cream so one, my half-Filipino son can appreciate foods inspired by the Philippines, and two, I could relive that summer day of discovery in New York City.

RECIPE SPECS

FOR THE ICE CREAM

7 ounces (200 g) sweet cream style corn, (about ½ of a 14¾ ounce, or 418 g can), heated in a heavy saucepan

About 1½ cups (352 g) cold heavy cream

3 tablespoons (24 g) confectioners' sugar

1 teaspoon vanilla extract

About ⅔ cup (200 g) sweetened condensed milk

⅓ cup (38 g) shredded cheddar cheese

About ¼ cup (35 g) pistachios (optional)

FOR THE BUTTERFLY PEA FLOWER SYRUP

¼ cup (50 g) granulated sugar

¼ cup (60 g) water

15 to 20 pieces of dried butterfly pea flowers (or 1 teaspoon butterfly pea flower powder)

1 Line a 9 x 5-inch (23 x 13 cm) loaf pan with plastic wrap that overhangs on all sides by at least 2 inches (5 cm).

2 *Make the ice cream.* In a saucepan, heat the sweet cream style corn until it simmers. Transfer to a blender or food processor and blend until puréed. Cool completely. In a stand mixer fitted with the whisk attachment, add the heavy cream and sugar. Beat on medium speed until soft peaks form. Add the vanilla extract and condensed milk and mix until thickened and smooth. Fold in the corn purée, cheese, and optional pistachios until evenly distributed across the mixture.

3 With a flexible spatula, scrape the ice cream mixture into the prepared loaf pan. Cover with plastic wrap and freeze for at least 6 hours or overnight.

4 *Make the butterfly pea flower syrup.* In a small saucepan, add all the ingredients and boil over high heat. Reduce the heat to medium and simmer the mixture until a thick syrup forms, about 5 to 6 minutes. Allow the syrup to cool at room temperature. Store in a glass jar or airtight container.

5 Let the ice cream soften for a few minutes at room temperature before serving on cones or in bowls. Drizzle with the blue butterfly pea flower syrup.

To make this a vegan ice cream, use vegan cheese, vegan condensed milk, and full-fat coconut milk from a can.

PREP TIME	15 MINUTES
INACTIVE TIME	4 TO 6 HOURS TO FREEZE THE ICE CREAM
COOK TIME	10 MINUTES FOR THE SYRUP
YIELD	1 LOAF PAN FULL OF ICE CREAM, FOR 4 TO 6 PEOPLE

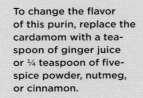

To change the flavor of this purin, replace the cardamom with a teaspoon of ginger juice or ¼ teaspoon of five-spice powder, nutmeg, or cinnamon.

Simply Perfect Purin

Michael Ruhlman, the author of *Ratio*, laments not enough people use butterscotch in their recipes anymore. So, here's a butterscotch caramel *purin* (or pudding) that's simply perfect.

Purin is a Japanese take on flan or crème caramel. You can find ready-made ones in any *konbini* (convenience store) across Japan. I love purin's smooth and creamy

texture. Each spoonful is a delightful marriage of sweet and bitter (thanks to the caramel).

Note: Because we'll be using a bain-marie, please have hot water, a baking pan, and four ramekins or pudding molds ready.

RECIPE SPECS

FOR THE BUTTERSCOTCH CARAMEL SAUCE

About ⅓ cup (67 g) packed brown sugar

1 tablespoon (15 g) water

½ tablespoon (7 g) unsalted or salted butter

Pinch of salt

Few drops of apple cider vinegar or lemon juice (optional)

FOR THE PURIN

1¾ cups (410 g) milk

3 medium eggs (about 5 ounces, or 150 g)

¼ cup (50 g) granulated sugar, adjust to taste

1 teaspoon vanilla extract

¼ teaspoon cardamom

FOR THE OPTIONAL GARNISHES

Whipped cream

Strawberries, cherries, or other fruits of choice

1 *Make the butterscotch caramel sauce.* In a small saucepan over medium heat, cook the brown sugar and water. Once the mixture thickens, add the butter, salt, and optional apple cider vinegar or lemon juice. Continue to heat the mixture until it turns golden amber (and not darker than that), when it reaches about 340°F to 345°F (171°C to 174°C). Remove from heat and quickly pour equal amounts into four 6-ounce (170 g) ramekins or pudding molds. Transfer the ramekins to the baking pan.

2 Preheat the oven to 310°F (155°C, or gas mark 2) and place a rack in the center.

3 *Make the purin.* Heat the milk over medium-high heat until small bubbles form on the edges of the milk. Alternatively, heat the milk in the microwave on high power for 90 seconds. The milk should be hot, but not boiling. Set aside.

4 In a large bowl, add the eggs, sugar, vanilla extract, and cardamom and whisk until combined.

5 Temper the eggs by adding a scoop of hot milk to the egg mixture while continuously whisking gently to combine. Continue to do this until you've added all the milk to the egg mixture to make the purin base. Strain the purin base with a fine-mesh sieve and pour evenly into the four ramekins.

6 Place the baking pan with the filled ramekins on the oven rack and pull the rack out. Fill the baking pan with hot water, about halfway up the sides of the ramekins.

7 Bake for 40 to 45 minutes, until the purin is almost set and the centers are jiggly but not runny.

8 Remove the ramekins from the oven and cool. Refrigerate for 4 hours or overnight.

9 Run a knife gently along the edges where the purin adheres to the ramekins and turn out onto serving plates. Garnish with optional whipped cream, strawberries, cherries, or other fruits of your choice.

PREP TIME	30 MINUTES
COOK TIME	50 TO 55 MINUTES
YIELD	4 PURIN

Choose long, slender sweet potatoes. You can use any type of sweet potato, but I've found the white-fleshed Japanese sweet potatoes to be the tastiest when baked this way.

Baked Sweet Potato Freezies

If you visit Asian cities during the wintertime, you'll come across street food vendors selling oozy, gooey delicious baked sweet potatoes, often cooked in woks. The high heat from the woks allows smoky magic to caramelize the potatoes. Chef Lucas Sin of Junzi Kitchen swears by freezing the potatoes first before baking them. He reasons that ice crystals within a frozen potato will mash its flesh while baking. Taiwanese vegan chef and a former moderator of SAB, George Lee, loves eating his baked potatoes frozen. It's a treat readily available in Taiwan's convenience stores. Lucas and George know what they're talking about, so I'm all for freezing the potatoes pre- and post-bake.

RECIPE SPECS

6 slender *satsumaimo* (Japanese white sweet potatoes)

Optional toppings such as butter or vegan butter, brown sugar, and cinnamon

1 Wash and scrub the potatoes clean and dry them thoroughly. Leave their skins intact. You do not need to use a fork to poke holes in the potatoes. Freeze the potatoes for 1 hour.

2 Preheat the oven to 455°F (235°C, or gas mark 8) and place a rack in the center. Line a large baking sheet with parchment paper.

3 Remove the potatoes from the freezer and transfer to the prepared baking sheet. Bake for about 70 minutes, until the skin darkens and caramelizes a bit.

4 Carefully remove the potatoes from the oven and cool for 10 minutes at room temperature. Cut the potatoes in half and serve with optional toppings such as butter or vegan butter and a sprinkling of brown sugar or cinnamon.

5 To enjoy the baked sweet potatoes as freezies, let them cool completely after baking. Freeze them for at least 3 hours. Then thaw them for 5 to 10 minutes before enjoying them cold.

PREP TIME	**5 MINUTES**
INACTIVE TIME	**1 HOUR FOR FREEZING (AND 3 HOURS AFTER BAKING, OPTIONAL)**
COOK TIME	**70 MINUTES**
YIELD	**6 FREEZIES**

Magical Ginger Milk Curd

This simple, fun, and magical Cantonese recipe is made with just three ingredients: ginger, milk, and sugar. Ginger is starchy, so it can curdle and thicken warm milk without help from thickening agents, making it magical! This spicy and slippery tofu-like dessert with a strong ginger taste is perfect on cold and gloomy days or on sick days when your throat's sore.

Note: Please note the milk's temperature will need to be precise, so have a candy or digital thermometer ready.

RECIPE SPECS

2 pieces of ginger, (4 inches, or 10 cm each), about 4 ounces (110 g) in total

About 1¾ cups (400 g) milk

1 to 2 tablespoons (13 to 26 g) granulated sugar, or to taste

1 teaspoon vanilla extract (optional)

1 Clean, dry, and peel the ginger. To extract the juice, cut up the ginger and squeeze out the juice using a garlic press. Sieve the juice through a fine-mesh strainer as needed. Alternatively, use a juicer to extract ginger juice.

2 Set out two serving bowls and add 1 tablespoon (15 g) of ginger juice to each bowl.

3 In a saucepan, add the milk, sugar, and optional vanilla extract. Whisk and heat the milk to 158°F to 167°F (70°C to 75°C). Remove from heat.

4 Stir the ginger juice. Quickly pour one half (200 g) of the warmed milk into each bowl, hitting the ginger juice. *Do not stir or mix* the mixture at this point. Allow the ginger milk curd to set and cool at room temperature, about 10 minutes.

5 Once the milk curd sets, it should hold the weight of a Chinese spoon (or any small spoon). Enjoy warm or chilled.

PREP TIME	**10 MINUTES**
INACTIVE TIME	**ABOUT 10 MINUTES**
COOK TIME	**10 MINUTES**
YIELD	**2 BOWLS**

Street Foods Mango Sticky Rice

Mango sticky rice (or *khao niao mamuang*) is a traditional Thai dessert popular across South and Southeast Asia. SAB member Liz O'Neill (@tatertotliz on Instagram) shared her mom's fantastic recipe and incredible story. Before immigrating to the United States, Liz's mom, Annie O'Neill, sold street foods in Cambodia and Vietnam during the Vietnam War. There she learned generations of cooking tips and tricks from her mother. Annie's mango sticky rice highlights the natural sweetness and richness of mangoes and coconut milk. Although mango sticky rice is relatively easy to make, Annie's recipe is extra non-fussy. You won't have to soak the glutinous rice overnight, as many other recipes require. Here is my adaptation of Annie's recipe.

RECIPE SPECS

FOR THE STICKY RICE

1 14-ounce can (400 g) full-fat coconut milk, refrigerated overnight

About 2 cups (380 g) glutinous rice

FOR THE COCONUT SAUCE

¼ teaspoon cornstarch

1 teaspoon water

3 tablespoons (39 g) granulated sugar

½ teaspoon salt

FOR THE TOPPINGS

2 to 3 ripe mangos, peeled, sliced, and chilled

Toasted sesame seeds (optional)

Dash of sea salt flakes (optional)

Thai basil, mint, or basil leave (optional)

1 *Make the sticky rice.* Transfer the separated, thick coconut cream from the can to a small saucepan. Set aside; keep the coconut liquid in the can.

2 Thoroughly wash the rice and soak in water for 1 hour. Drain the rice, add a pinch of salt, and steam it over medium heat and boiling water for 40 to 45 minutes, until tender. Every 5 minutes, carefully drizzle coconut liquid all over the rice, a few tablespoons (45 to 60 g) at a time, until the can is empty. Be sure to check the water level of the pot or wok periodically and replenish with hot water as needed.

3 You can also cook the rice in a multi-cooker or rice cooker. If you do, add all the coconut liquid and the required amount of water to the rice before cooking.

4 As the rice is cooking, *make the coconut sauce.* In a small bowl, mix and dissolve the cornstarch in the water. In the saucepan with the coconut cream, add the sugar and salt. Cook over medium-low heat until it simmers. Add the cornstarch water and stir. Reduce the heat to low and cook until you've got the thickened sauce consistency you like, about 1 to 2 minutes.

5 Once the rice is ready, mix it with half of the coconut sauce. Divide the rice into four equal portions and transfer to serving plates. Decorate the rice with the prepared mangos and serve with the remaining coconut sauce, drizzled over the mangos. If desired, sprinkle some sesame seeds and a dash of sea salt flakes on top of the coconut sauce and garnish with fragrant herb leaves.

Mango sticky rice is amazing when it's still warm. You can also enjoy it chilled.

> If you're using a rice cooker, only soak the rice for 15 minutes.

PREP TIME	**10 MINUTES**
INACTIVE TIME	**60 MINUTES**
COOK TIME	**40 TO 45 MINUTES**
YIELD	**4 SERVINGS**

Omit the black tea bags and use 1 tablespoon (6 g) of matcha to make a matcha version. Or try using different flavored tea in bags.

Mochi Boba Milk Tea Ice Pops

Need a treat that's perfect for kiddos and boba tea lovers on hot summer days? Try this recipe to make a frozen brown sugar boba tea. As tapioca boba will harden into pebbles when frozen, we'll be making mochi boba.

RECIPE SPECS

FOR THE TEA CREAM AND ICE POP BASE

1¾ cup (420 g) heavy cream

2 high-quality black tea bags

FOR THE BROWN SUGAR SYRUP

1 tablespoon (15 g) packed dark brown sugar

FOR THE MOCHI BOBA PEARLS

½ cup plus 2 tablespoons (75 g) glutinous rice flour, plus more for dusting work surface, divided

¼ cup (60 g) packed dark brown sugar

¼ cup (60 g) boiling water (add more water if the dough is too dry)

FOR THE BROWN SUGAR WATER MIXTURE

¾ cup (about 170 g) dark brown sugar

1½ cups (about 355 g) water

FOR THE ICE POP BASE

½ cup plus 1 tablespoon (about 120 g) sweetened condensed milk

1 teaspoon vanilla extract

Pinch of salt

PREP TIME	35 MINUTES
INACTIVE TIME	OVERNIGHT, FOR CHILLING AND FREEZING
COOK TIME	35 MINUTES
YIELD	4 TO 6 ICE POPS, DEPENDING ON THE SIZE OF THE MOLDS

1 *Make the tea cream.* In a saucepan, add the heavy cream, tea bags, and dark brown sugar. Simmer over medium-low heat for a few minutes. Remove from heat. Allow the tea bags to steep for 30 minutes before removing them. Cover and refrigerate overnight.

2 *Make the mochi boba pearls.* In a large bowl, combine ½ cup (60 g) of the flour and the dark brown sugar. Drizzle the boiling water over the mixture, stir to combine, and cool.

3 Add the remaining 2 tablespoons (15 g) of the glutinous rice flour to a medium bowl and set aside.

4 Transfer the mochi boba pearls to a floured work surface and knead until a dough forms. Pinch off a small piece of dough, about ¼ inch (6 mm) in diameter, and shape into a ball (boba). Drop into the bowl with the rice flour. Repeat with the remaining mochi dough. Keep any dough you're not working with covered with a damp towel.

5 Roll all the mochi boba around in the bowl to coat with glutinous rice flour. Transfer to a fine-mesh strainer to sift off the extra flour.

6 In a pot, boil 4 to 5 cups (940 g to 1.2 kg) of water. Transfer the boba to the pot and boil for 3 minutes, until the boba float to the surface. Strain.

7 *Make the brown sugar water mixture.* In a large pot, add the ingredients and mix. Bring to a boil while mixing continuously, and then reduce the heat to low. Pour in the mochi boba and simmer for a few minutes while continuously stirring. Use a slotted spoon to remove the boba from the sugar water and set aside to cool.

8 *Make the ice pop base.* In a stand mixer fitted with the whisk attachment, beat the chilled tea cream until soft peaks form, a few minutes. Add the condensed milk, vanilla extract, and salt and beat until combined and thickened. Add the boba to the cream and gently mix until evenly distributed. Scoop the ice pop base into the molds. Stir each with a skewer or chopsticks to get rid of air bubbles.

9 Freeze the ice pops for at least 5 hours.

10 Unmold the ice pops and consume within 1 to 2 days. The mochi boba will harden dramatically after the second day of freezing.

Effortless Matcha Chia Pudding

I love starting busy mornings with a jar of this matcha chia pudding. It's so effortless to make, plus matcha provides a boost of caffeine, making this dish perfect for breakfast or brunch.

To make matcha overnight oats instead, replace the chia seeds with ¾ cup (54 g) rolled oats.

RECIPE SPECS

2 tablespoons (26 g) chia seeds

1 cup (235 g) milk of choice

1 to 2 teaspoons matcha

1 to 2 tablespoons liquid sweetener, such as (20 to 40 g) honey, (20 to 40 g) maple syrup, (22 to 44 g) agave syrup, or (19 to 38 g) sweetened condensed milk, adjust to taste

¼ teaspoon miso (optional)

1 teaspoon vanilla extract (optional)

1 ripe banana, mashed

1 Except for the mashed banana, add all the ingredients, including the optional ones, to a medium bowl and combine. Yeap, that's it.

2 Cover and refrigerate the chia pudding mixture overnight or for at least 2 hours. The mixture will thicken beautifully after about 2 hours of refrigeration.

3 Add the mashed banana and stir. Serve in a jar or bowl.

Alternatively, with parfait glasses, you can make matcha chia pudding parfait. Using your favorite Greek yogurt and berries of choice, create parfait layers with the chia pudding. Start with a layer of the chia pudding, then a layer of yogurt, and then a layer of berries. Repeat and enjoy.

Recipe tester Mimi Truong recommends going wild with your imagination to see what else you can put in your matcha chia pudding.

PREP TIME	5 MINUTES
INACTIVE TIME	2 HOURS TO OVERNIGHT TO CHILL
YIELD	1 BOWL

Drinks

The drink recipes here are steeped in nostalgia for me. All throughout the 1990s to the early 2000s, whenever my dad took us to a Vietnamese restaurant, he would order a Vietnamese coffee. I loved sneaking sips of his coffee even though I'd be buzzed all night! Now I make my own Vietnamese coffee at home with a phin filter. You can too, but with a twist, with my Vietnamese Egg Dalgona Coffee recipe (page 164).

Although Mom and I never made cupcakes, cookies, and frosting together, she did make a lot of comforting Cantonese sweet soups and drinks. It doesn't matter what the weather is like outside or how I'm feeling—I loved making smooth and refreshing Homemade Soy Milk (page 168) with her. These days, I make it with my son.

Two recipes here, Suraj's Lemongrass Chai Latte (page 162) and my Mango Lassi with Sago (page 170) are a homage to Indian cuisine. Indian food is so comforting to me. When we moved across the country from New York to Washington state, we knew no one and had no one. Our first friends in the Seattle area were Indian families (Mary Usha Kachana's, Deepthi Prasad's, and Suraj Chetnani's families) who welcomed us and continuously shower us with amazing homemade Indian food and their love, for which we are forever grateful.

Every recipe in this section has a story and is personal to me. I hope these drinks refresh you, comfort you, and bring you lots of delight, my dear friend. Change them up as you desire and make them a part of your story.

Suraj's Lemongrass Chai Latte

My good friend, Suraj Chetnani, loves to serve us this chai latte whenever my family visits his home. I've joked we would stop coming over if he stops making chai for us! What makes Suraj's chai unique is that he uses fresh lemongrass, giving it a hint of citrus.

As he sips chai, Suraj thinks of his *nani* (grandmother). He fondly recounts his afternoons in Mumbai when they enjoyed chai together while eating different Indian snacks. Nani liked her chai super sweet and would usually put 4 teaspoons of sugar in her cup. She would pour it on a small plate to cool it down and sip it from there.

Typical *masala* (or blend of spices) added in chai include cardamom, cloves, nutmeg, coriander, cinnamon, and pepper. In India, every family has unique masala they prefer in their chai. This lemongrass chai is Suraj's chai.

RECIPE SPECS

1 cup (235 g) water

About ⅔ cup (157 g) milk

2 inch (5 cm)-long piece of lemongrass, the green parts only, chopped

½ teaspoon grated ginger (optional)

2 teaspoons Indian brand tea or your best black tea

1 teaspoon brown sugar, adjust to taste

1 Add all the ingredients to a saucepan or small pot and cook on medium-high heat. Stir once every minute for 4 to 5 minutes. When the milk starts rising, quickly lower the heat to medium-low and simmer for 7 to 8 minutes while stirring every minute. Use a fine-mesh strainer to sieve the chai into a serving cup (or divide evenly between two cups).

2 Sip your chai while it's warm. Serve with snacks such as samosa or biscuits.

To make vegan chai, replace the milk with plant-based milk. Bring only the water to a boil first before adding all the dry ingredients. Simmer for 4 to 5 minutes. Remove from the heat. Then, add the desired amount of plant-based milk. To make iced chai, use this version of the recipe and add ice at the end.

PREP TIME	**5 MINUTES**
COOK TIME	**11 TO 13 MINUTES**
YIELD	**TEA FOR 2 OR FOR 1 CHAI LOVER**

Vietnamese Egg Dalgona Coffee

In 1946, when fresh milk was in short supply across Vietnam, the owner of Cafe Giảng in Hanoi concocted Vietnamese Egg Coffee (*Cà Phê Trứng*). As for Dalgona coffee, it's an early COVID-19 pandemic quarantine viral trend that circulated worldwide from South Korea. It is named dalgona after a sweet Korean street food: dalgona or honeycomb toffee.

Now, we can finally stop comparing these two drinks to each other when we can have the best of both worlds with this delicious and easy-to-make mixture.

Note: Dalgona coffee always uses a 1:1:1 ratio of instant coffee to hot water to sugar.

FOR THE EGG MIXTURE

1 pasteurized egg yolk (about ¾ ounce, or 20 g)

2 tablespoons (38 g) sweetened condensed milk

OTHER INGREDIENTS

½ cup plus 1 tablespoon (135 g) milk of choice

1 teaspoon cocoa powder (optional)

FOR THE DALGONA MIXTURE

2 tablespoons (26 g) granulated sugar

2 tablespoons (30 g) hot water

2 tablespoons (6 g) instant coffee

1 *Make the egg mixture.* In a stand mixer fitted with the whisk attachment, add the egg yolk. Beat on high speed for 1 to 2 minutes. Add the condensed milk and beat on high speed for about 3 minutes, until light and fluffy.

2 Fill two tall glasses halfway with ice. Pour in your milk of choice to fill about two-thirds of each glass. Divide the egg mixture evenly into the glasses.

3 *Make the dalgona mixture.* Beat the sugar, hot water, and instant coffee on high speed for about 5 minutes, until you get stiff peaks. Scoop generous amounts of the dalgona on top of the egg mixture. Dust with the cocoa powder.

4 Stir gently with a spoon or straw.

PREP TIME	**5 MINUTES**
COOK TIME	**10 MINUTES**
YIELD	**2 GLASSES**

SAB's
Pink Drink

This pretty and refreshing drink is perfect on melty summer days or whenever you're craving a soda but want something a bit healthier and, well, naturally pink.

Feel free to add more than one bottle of Yakult to this drink. Yakult is a probiotic milk beverage from Japan, easily found in Asian markets and many Western markets these days. If it's hard to get your hands on some Yakult, use kefir or a thin liquid yogurt instead.

RECIPE SPECS

5 to 6 strawberries

7 to 8 raspberries

1 tablespoon (13 g) granulated sugar, adjust to taste

¼ cup (60 g) water

2 teaspoons sweetened condensed milk

Ice cubes

Unflavored seltzer or sparkling water of choice

1 bottle (2.7 ounces, or 80 ml) Yakult

1 tablespoon (1 g) freeze-dried strawberries (optional)

1 Combine the fresh strawberries, raspberries, sugar, and water in a blender. Blend until smooth and puréed.

2 Dip a spoon into the condensed milk. Using the back of the coated spoon, swirl and coat the entire inside of two tall glasses, from bottom to top.

3 Divide and pour the purée into the glasses.

4 Add the ice cubes three-fourths the way up the glass. Leaving room for the Yakult, add seltzer water to the glasses. Add the Yakult, aiming for the ice cubes. Add the optional freeze-dried strawberries. There will be a beautiful layering of the ingredients in the drink. It's up to you whether you'd like to stir before serving and drinking. Drink pink and let me know what you think!

Want to try something eggciting? In a small bowl, whisk together a pasteurized egg yolk and 1 to 2 tablespoons (19 to 38 g) of sweetened condensed milk. Once well-incorporated and fluffy, add it to your pink drink, replacing the Yakult (or keep the Yakult!). This variation of the SAB's Pink Drink would be my riff on Vietnamese Egg Soda.

PREP TIME	10 MINUTES
YIELD	2 GLASSES

Homemade Soy Milk

Back in Coney Island, where I grew up in Brooklyn, Mom and I used to make soy milk in large batches. I was in charge of soaking the soybeans overnight. The next day, Mom and I would blend the soybeans and strain their pulp (or *okara*) with old (but clean!) pantyhose. (Hey, why buy cheesecloth when we had something we could use at home, right?)

We gave our delicious homemade soy milk to our neighbors. One neighbor developed a terrible rash and discovered he was allergic to unprocessed soy milk. Still, he drank down every last drop! Bless his heart. *(Please don't do that if you have a soy allergy.)*

RECIPE SPECS

1 cup (186 g) soybeans

1 tablespoon (8 g) toasted sesame seeds (optional)

6 cups (1410 g) filtered water

½ teaspoon salt or ¼ teaspoon miso

1 teaspoon vanilla extract (optional)

Granulated sugar, adjust to taste (optional)

1 Wash and soak the soybeans overnight.

2 Drain the water from the soybeans. In a blender, add the soybeans, optional sesame seeds, and filtered water. Blend on high speed for about 1 minute until you get a fine mixture.

3 Pour the mixture into a large pot and boil over medium heat. Stir occasionally, so the soybean okara does not burn. Add the salt. Reduce the heat to medium-low and simmer the mixture for 15 to 20 minutes, occasionally stirring. The soy milk will thicken slightly.

4 If making sweetened soy milk, add the optional vanilla extract and sugar to taste. For unsweetened soy milk, omit the vanilla extract and sugar. For a salty soy milk, just add more salt or miso to taste. Remove from heat and cool completely.

5 Strain the mixture with cheesecloth or a fine-mesh sieve. (If you have clean pantyhose, that works too!)

6 Serve or refrigerate for at least 4 hours to enjoy cold. Store for up to 4 days in the refrigerator.

The legendary Maangchi of maangchi.com recommends adding unsalted roasted cashews, peanuts, walnuts, or even pine nuts to the blender to elevate homemade soy milk.

PREP TIME	**5 MINUTES**
COOK TIME	**25 MINUTES**
YIELD	**4 GLASSES**

Mango Lassi
with Sago

One of my favorite desserts originating from Hong Kong is mango *pomelo sago*, and my go-to Indian drink is the classic mango lassi. So, I thought, why not combine the two and make a whole new recipe? The resulting combo is a tasty mango lassi with sago. It's a fun, not-too-sweet, and textured drink that's incredibly refreshing during the summertime. Or have it while eating spicy foods. Your mouth will thank you.

Note: Sago pearls are tiny and transparent boba pearls that are different from tapioca pearls. Sago comes from the inner part of a sago palm tree, and tapioca comes from cassava roots. Tapioca pearls are the chewier of the two.

RECIPE SPECS

About ¼ cup (45 g)
uncooked sago pearls

FOR THE MANGO LASSI

1 cup (175 g) diced
ripe mango

1 cup (230 g) plain
yogurt or Greek yogurt

½ cup (120 g) milk

1 tablespoon (13 g)
granulated sugar or
(20 g) honey, to taste

¼ teaspoon ground
cardamom or cinnamon,
to taste (optional)

FOR THE OPTIONAL TOPPINGS

¼ cup (60 g) full-fat
coconut milk (optional)

Pinch of saffron or
1 tablespoon (8 g)
chopped pistachios for
garnishing (optional)

1 In a large pot, bring 5 cups (1.2 kg) of water to a boil. Add the sago and cook over medium heat for 15 to 20 minutes, until they are completely translucent. Drain the sago and run under cold water for a few seconds. Set aside.

2 *Make the mango lassi.* Add the mango, yogurt, milk, sugar or honey, and optional cardamom or cinnamon to a blender. If you like your drinks cold, add a few ice cubes. Blend until smooth and puréed.

3 *Assemble your drink.* Add a few teaspoons (about 20 g) of sago pearls into a tall serving glass. Leaving one-fourth of the glass empty, pour in the mango lassi. Optionally, top with half of the coconut milk. If desired, garnish with a pinch of saffron or some chopped pistachios or both. Repeat with the second serving glass.

4 Give it a good stir and enjoy this drink with a loved one.

If you have pomelo (a large citrus fruit from Southeast Asia that tastes like mild grapefruit), try mixing in a few spoonfuls of its pulp to this drink.

Mango lassi can be enjoyed frozen as ice pops! Just pour the mango lassi into reusable ice pop molds and freeze for a few hours.

PREP TIME	10 MINUTES
COOK TIME	15 TO 20 MINUTES (TO BOIL THE SAGO)
YIELD	2 TALL GLASSES

Acknowledgments

To my husband and son: Jake and Phil, words will never adequately express how much I love and appreciate you both. Your support and love have helped me achieve one of my lifelong dreams.

To my parents: Mom and Dad, thank you for everything. And Dad, I hope there are lots of sweets in heaven for you to enjoy.

To my recipe testers: Thank you for your precious time and invaluable feedback and insights. Without you, this cookbook could not have been completed! To each one of you, I am forever grateful.

Belén Barbed

Gloria Deng

Rachel Emily Isabella Galvin

Rachel Gascon

Gayatri Das Gupta

Ingrid Koo

Sabrina Koo

Jen Lee

Tony P. Liao

Susan H. Louangsaysongkham

Tran Nguyen

Liza Thuy Nguyen

Hannah Park

Camille Ramos

Jonni Scott

Anthea Tang

Melinda Trang

Mimi Truong

Francine Tychuaco

Sarah H. Ung

Tiffany Voon

Jina Yee

Sharon Yeung

To the wonderful SAB Community, my SAB Fam, this is our book.

To the SAB Team: Ashley Howard, Owen Li, Will Leung, Noelle Peterson, and Sharon Yeung, thank you for helping build and manage the SAB Community. Thank you also to former SAB moderators George Lee and Nichole Tan.

To the team at Quarry Books: Jonathan Simcosky, Anne Re, Joy Aquilino, Todd Conly, Elizabeth Weeks, Marilyn Kecyk, and the Quarry Books team, I'm so grateful to have worked on my first cookbook with you!

To Nicole and Jeff Soper: You made this book come alive with your beautiful pictures! I loved watching you work, meticulously style all my recipes, and put your love and heart into each photo.

To Eater: Thank you to Erin DeJesus and Eater for publishing a wonderful article by the amazing writer Jessica Wei featuring SAB and the SAB Community.

To the Subtle Asian Traits (SAT) Community: Thank you, SAT Team, for paving the way online, especially for Asian creators around the globe.

Last—but not least— I thank you, the reader.
<3

About the Author

KAT LIEU, *formerly a doctor of physical therapy, fell in love with baking. She is currently a full-time author and recipe developer at modernasianbaking.com. Originally from New York, she now calls Washington state her home. Lieu is also the founder of a popular online baking group called Subtle Asian Baking (SAB). You can find more of her recipes and creations on her Instagram and TikTok, @subtleasian.baking.*

Index